Mysticism and Poetry

DR. ALLEN BROCKINGTON
From a painting by Will. C. Penn, R.O.I.

Mysticism and Poetry
On a Basis of Experience

by
A. Allen Brockington

With a Foreword by
Sir Arthur Eddington

Ex spinis uvas

KENNIKAT PRESS
Port Washington, N. Y./London

MYSTICISM AND POETRY

First published in 1934
Reissued in 1970 by Kennikat Press
Library of Congress Catalog Card No: 74-105767
ISBN 0-8046-1044-4

Manufactured by Taylor Publishing Company   Dallas, Texas

To
THE MEMORY
OF
MY FATHER

FOREWORD

IN his autobiographical account of the growth of
his own mystical outlook, Dr. Brockington refers
(p. 15) to his acceptance of a mastership at a
small school in the neighbourhood of his old haunts.
This was in a period of his life which he passes over
briefly as though relatively empty of spiritual growth;
and he does not even mention that, although called
away after one term, he not long afterwards returned
to be headmaster of the same school. To me the
incident had more importance; for it meant the trans-
formation of those wearisome school-hours devoted
to English into a time of joy and revelation. Our
class was too young to respond easily and instinct-
ively to the appeal of the poets and the great prose-
writers; it was the personality and enthusiasm of the
master that illumined the field of English literature
for us. He not merely opened the door; he swept us
through with him. Those who read this book will, I
think, feel something of the same spell that he
exercised on me nearly forty years ago.

Were it not for this relationship of pupil and
master, it would seem an impertinence for me casually
to put together a few paragraphs to set alongside a
work which is the fruit of life-long study. As a

Quaker the deeper side of mysticism is not foreign to me; and my very occasional writing on the subject is represented by quotations which appear in this book. But it is with regard to the more circuitous approach to the mystic frontiers through physical science that I may chiefly venture to speak. The handling of mysticism by a scientist (if he keeps strictly to his science) cannot go very far. It is perhaps to be regarded as Dr. Johnson regarded a dog's walking on his hind legs : " It is not done well : but you are surprised to find it done at all." I know of no better summary of the present scientific outlook, as I conceive it, than the statement of one of the greatest living mathematicians, Hermann Weyl :—

> Modern science, in so far as I am familiar with it through my own scientific work, mathematics and physics, makes the world appear more and more as an open one, as a world not closed but pointing beyond itself . . . Science finds itself compelled, at once by the epistemological, the physical and the constructive-mathematical aspect of its own methods and results, to recognise this situation. It remains to be added that science can do no more than show us this open horizon; we must not attempt to establish anew a closed (though more comprehensive) world.

The last sentence is to be stressed. Physical science is by its own implications led to *recognise* a domain of experience beyond its frontiers, but not to *annex* it. All varieties of mysticism represent an escape from the closed world of physics into the open world beyond it and to which it points. But just because mysticism concerns an experience beyond physics, we must not call in physical science to guarantee it or to confirm our interpretation of it. That would be to bow our necks again to the yoke from which we have escaped.

He who views mysticism from the standpoint of scientific philosophy may be compared to a man looking down on a city from a height. He may grasp better than the dweller in the city the lie of the land, and see how the features blend into the surrounding country. It is something that, from the present peak of science, the clouds have so far rolled away that we seem able to make out the site of the city, or, in Weyl's metaphor, we discern the open horizon. But the domain thus revealed ought to be known from within. To join in this knowledge we must surrender our scientific vantage point, and enter the way by which man has from the earliest times entered into the things of the spirit. We must be of the fellowship of those who speak to us in the pages of this book.

A. S. E.

CONTENTS

PART I : INTRODUCTION.

PART II : VISION.

PART IV: INTUITION.

PART V: THE TRADITIONAL VIEW OF MYSTICISM.

I

INTRODUCTION

I

INTRODUCTION

I BEGAN this piece of writing with the notion that there was a mystical element of poetry and that this element could be studied adequately in some English poems. I was familiar with Vision (in the technical sense) and ' Dictation ' (in Blake's sense) and also with Intuition; and I set out to examine and illustrate these modes of apprehension. I had no feeling, then, that I was examining anything unknown to the majority of men or not understood by them. Or, perhaps, it would be truer to say that I considered Intuition to be a universal endowment of man, and Vision to be an occasional experience in the lives of many men and women, and Dictation to be a common experience of poets. My conviction was that both Vision and Dictation should be regarded as forms of Intuition.

It did not strike me as necessary to *prove* that there was another kind of ' thought ' (*pensée*) than abstract and discursive thought and another kind of knowledge than conceptual or rational knowledge until I read Henri Bremond's *Prière et Poésie*.[1] This book was a turning-point in my investigations. It served to stress my determination to deal as fully as

[1] Grasset (Paris) 23e Edition.

3

possible with modes of apprehension, especially as the brilliant and learned author seemed to agree with the conclusion I had already reached : that Intuition was the mode of apprehension essential to the mystical life. But his view of Mysticism was of devotional mysticism.

One purpose of *Prière et Poésie* is to show that the poet's ' poetic experience ' is a kind of prayer, and that this poetic experience may be enjoyed by those who listen to poetry. In other words, that hearing poetry starts the psychological mechanism of prayer, and that in favourable conditions the prayer, so started, will lead on to the highest end of true prayer. The highest end is the ' mystical experience.'

Bremond's treatment of the ' poetic experience ' is based upon a study of mysticism. *Prière*, of the title, is mysticism. The mystical experience is an experience of prayer.

He speaks of another sort of mysticism, ' *la mystique naturelle*,' or, as it is sometimes called, ' *la mystique profane*.' Of natural mysticism he says, in a footnote [1] :

' A parler en toute rigeur, il n'y a pas de " mystique naturelle " dans l'ordre historique où nous sommes placés, l'ordre de la Rédemption. Tous les hommes ont une même fin surnaturelle, la vision béatifique. Sauver—et ils peuvent l'être—un païen d'avant le Christ ou d'aujourd'hui, ont la même récompense essentielle que les saints canonisés. D'où il suit que tous les secours que Dieu nous offre ont toujours pour fin suprême de nous conduire à la vision béati-

[1] *op. cit.* p. 109.

fique. D'un autre côté, comment ne pas reconnaître dans les inspirations véritables, autant de secours prévus de toute éternité et voulus par Dieu, autant de ' moyens de salut,' et, enfin, autant de ' grâces.' Nous savons du reste, que, le Christ étant mort pour tous, la grâce de la conversion n'est refusée à personne. Or, qui ne voit que le mécanisme de ' l'inspiration ' tel que nous l'avons décrit, s'adapte merveilleusement aux interventions divines dans notre vie, aux touches, aux motions divines ? . . . . Et voici qui nous permet encore d'appeler ' graces,' certaines inspirations dans l'analyse desquelles, on se refuserait—témérairement peut-être—à reconnaître une de ces motions divines.'

This was the first clear recognition [1] I had seen of the same mode of apprehension as applying to *la mystique naturelle* and to *la haute vie mystique proprement dite,* though Bremond is careful to remind his readers that the mystical states of the poet and hero, as such, are not the ' state of grace.'

I was ready enough to admit that the impassioned intuition of Shelley (say) differed profoundly from the ' intuition of God as present,' [2] which is the typical experience of the contemplative. At the same time I was anxious to make clear to myself :

(1). In what way and in what precise sense *mystique* had come to be attached to *la haute vie;*

---

[1] *cf.* Auguste Sandreau in *L'État Mystique* (Second Edition 1921), quoting Dionysius the Areopagite : ' Cette science est bien supérieure à celle que nous pouvons obtenir par les lumières de notre raison. Par notre raison, en effet nous ne connaissons le divin que dans ses effets ; mais de dire ce qu'il est en Lui-même, c'est ce qui dépasse tout entendement . . .' p. 22.

[2] Bremond *op. cit.* p. 143.

(2). In what way *la mystique naturelle* had originated, and in what sense this state or experience was called mystical.

But what thread should I follow? And suddenly I resolved to follow the thread of my own experiences. My first salient experience came in the hearing of a great poem. I knew what Vision was from my own experience. I had written both prose and verse in the manner indicated by Blake.[1] My later experiences, especially during and immediately after the War, were much concerned with praying and with dictated or intuitive [2] decisions. These facts of experience were the facts of an insignificant person, but all the older writers about mysticism had proceeded on a basis of fact, and I might find my advantage in doing the same. Accordingly, I wrote down the appended autobiographical details. I must apologise for the record of early impressions—they are only substantially accurate—and, in particular, for a *verbatim* report of a conversation with my father. I remember this talk very vividly, but I cannot claim that the wording is exact or that the allusion to Hotspur's death was supported by precise quotation. I think

[1] For specimens (anonymous) see *The Nation: Home Again*, June 1, 1918; *The News*, Sept. 28, 1918; *Ariel*, Dec. 14, 1918; *The Poet's Wife*, July 31, 1920; and *The Nation* (New York): *Youth Passes*, Nov. 4, 1919 (signed).

[2] *cf. The Man of Science and the Science of Man* by J. L. Myres, p. 41: 'For in living, as we all know to our cost, especially when our training has been predominantly intellectual, the final decision is given not by reason but by sensibility. It may be, and often is, the right decision; but of this we satisfy ourselves intellectually in retrospect. But at the time it was not merely and sheerly a rational act.' Keats said that poetry should 'come' as 'naturally' as leaves to a tree. Wordsworth held that 'intuitive truths' were the highest. J. S. Mill called Carlyle a 'man of intuition.' Even Walter Hilton means intuition when he talks of the 'reformation of feeling' (*Scale of Perfection* Pt. II). 'Sensibility,' 'Inspiration,' 'Intuition' are words for the same thing.

my father said, ' Time must have a stop,' and my full
amazement came later when I looked up the passage.

I

I was only a small boy, though I forget my age,
when my father said to me, after some talk of Sir
Walter Scott, ' Would you like to hear some real
poetry? ' I was a little resentful of his question and
his tone. I thought my beloved Sir Walter wrote
' real ' poetry. I submitted, however, and said
rather grudgingly, ' Yes, I should.' He told me to
sit down and listen. He read Coleridge's *Ancient
Mariner*. Very soon something was happening
inside me which had never happened before.

> The fair breeze blew, the white foam flew,
>   The furrow followed free;
> We were the first that ever burst
>   Into that silent sea.
>
> Down dropt the breeze, the sails dropt down,
>   'Twas sad as sad could be;
> And we did speak only to break
>   The silence of the sea.
>
> Fly, brother, fly more high, more high,
>   Or we shall be belated.
>
>   O happy living things!
>
> A noise like as of a hidden brook
>   In the leafy month of June,
> That to the sleeping woods all night
>   Singeth a quiet tune.
>
> And the coming wind did roar more loud
>   And the sails did sigh like sedge
> And the rain poured down from one black cloud;
>   The moon was at its edge.
>
> And on the bay the moonlight lay
>   And the shadow of the moon.

These were the things that stayed with me. The silent, silent sea and the ship bursting into it. I knew that the ship could not burst into any real sea. This was the sea as it seemed to the mind, so inexpressibly silent that a ship sailing into it was a crash, and so sad, nothing sadder, that the sad men only spoke to break its silence. And, oh, the quiet tune of the hidden brook, the tune I knew already and had wondered at, and the woods lulled to sleep by it! The shadow of the moon! What did he mean by that? I did not care what he meant. The moon at the edge of the black cloud. But the music of the words! How was it said? I longed to say something like it.

After that I began to carry Palgrave's *Golden Treasury* in my pocket and read it in secret. I learned Shelley's *Skylark*. I loved

> In profuse strains of unpremeditated art.

I think I loved all the long verses at the end of stanzas.

' Our sweetest songs are those that tell of saddest thought.' Yet there were ' happy living things,' I used to taste that over and over again. And, later on, I remembered

> Around, around flew each sweet sound . . .

We lived in an ordinary street in a large town. Sometimes I did not care where we lived. My father became an invalid. Sometimes I was glad that he was confined to the house because I could be sure of finding him there. He was devoted to music. He had a ' reedy ' voice of great compass and even when he was ill he sang sometimes. He repeated tunes and phrases that I vaguely remembered hearing him sing when I was a mere toddler: ' Here in this sacred dwelling . . . . ' from the *Magic Flute* and the German folk-song, *The Millwheel*.

I learned to play the piano—not well, but well enough to get through the piano-accompaniment of things like *Don Giovanni*. While I played he sat in a deep arm-chair and ' sang the tunes in his mind,' he told me. He discarded old loves: *Elijah*, for one. Haydn he called ' milk for babes.' Wagner he hardly lived to know; he reached us too late. ' When I was a boy,' he said to me once, ' I used to save up my money to go to Chamber Concerts.' That was my father. What he was to others I hardly knew. We *were* the stuff that dreams are made on.

He became a reader of Emerson (whose chosen mystic is Swedenborg), of his poems as well as of his essays. One phrase from Emerson he quoted frequently: a man must not be a ' mush of concession '—something different from being a ' pushed peach ' to the touch of the right teacher. He dwelt also on Emerson's account of seeing *Hamlet*. Emerson followed the play until he heard the verse:

Revisit'st thus the glimpses of the moon

and then sat back and ' tasted ' the verse for the rest of the evening. This was my father's impression. Emerson does not use the word ' tasted.' [1] I looked up the context and found it to be:

[1] Shakespeare : or the Poet

That thou, dead corse, again, in complete steel,
Revisit'st thus the glimpses of the moon,
Making night hideous; and we fools of nature
So horridly to shake our dispositions
With thoughts beyond the reaches of our souls.

But, at that time, my father and I had glimpses of the moon that made night splendid, and though the thoughts beyond the reaches of our souls may have shaken our dispositions they did not shake them horridly.

The next enormous event was Plato's *Phaedo*. I am glad he lived until the *Phaedo* arrived in our lives. I was the reader this time. I used to run all the way home to tell him about it : first, the discovery of what I conceived to be Christianity before Christ came; and, next, the proof of the immortality of the soul. We were both much excited. After long pondering he said, ' I like Plato's theory of Ideas. But have we an idea of a circle behind the actual circles we draw ? We have an idea of a Man because the Man has come.' Someone told me of the *Republic*, and I read the well-known passage [1] of the man who wished to *be* and not to *seem* just, and the prediction that he would be crucified.

' Yes,' he said, ' that is Plato's man but he is not Christ.' I reminded him of St. John's Prologue : ' In the beginning was the Word . . . and the Word was made Flesh.' He answered : ' Plato argues that we pre-existed, and that, if we pre-existed, we must therefore continue to exist after death. Christ brought life and immortality to light through the Gospel.'

I said, ' You believe in the immortality of the soul ? '

[1] Republic II, 361 [Glaucon].

He said, ' Not unconditionally. The soul is not automatically immortal.'

' You believe that you will be living after you have died ? '

' I have a feeling that I shall.'

' Why ? '

' Why have I a feeling ? ' He laughed. ' How can anyone tell why he has a feeling ? The feeling comes.'

' I meant, what will you be living for ? '

' I suppose, to be used.'

' Happily ? Shall you be happy ? '

' Of course.'

' Christ pre-existed.'

' Yes,' he said, ' but Christ is God.'

' All the time ? '

' There is no question of time.'

' He was born " in time." '

' For us men and for our salvation. We are creatures of time. But time, as Hotspur says, must have a stop.'

' Hotspur ? '

' Yes. Just before he died :—

> But thought's the slave of life, and life's time's fool;
> And time, which takes survey of all the world,
> Must have a stop.'

I looked at him in amazement. I felt we were being transported beyond the limits of everything. Time must have a stop ! Truth sits upon the lips of dying men. My father was slowly dying. He knew it. But what—what—what did Hotspur mean ? Is thought the slave of life ? Thought is. There is something more than thought. My father had a feeling that he would be living after his death. His feeling was more than thought. And he knew why he would be living : to be used. That was something definitely *not* the slave of life. And when time had a stop you would not be living in terms of time, though you might survey it, even as time now surveyed the world.

' Well ! ' he said, at length, ' I am not dead yet.'

I left him to do some work as a tutor. I developed some minor ailment, which he mistook for a serious illness. He sent me a packet of stamped and addressed postcards, so that he could hear every day how I was.

My work lay in a lovely part of England. In the Summer I used to wander over the hills, softly-rounded, with combes dividing the ridges, well-watered, Coleridge's country, where those brooks sing their quiet tunes. I saw the amphitheatre which seemed to him ' like society.' I saw his cottage where he wrote the *Ancient Mariner*. I read, in the very room he was speaking of, his *Frost at Midnight*, and that for the first time :—

> . . . Sea, and hill, and wood,
> With all the numberless goings-on of life
> Inaudible as dreams ! the thin blue flame
> Lies on my low burnt fire, and quivers not;
> Only that film, which fluttered on the grate,
> Still flutters there, the sole unquiet thing.
> Methinks, its motion in the hush of nature
> Gives it dim sympathies with me who live,
> Making it a companionable form,
> Whose puny flaps and freaks the idling Spirit
> By its own moods interprets, everywhere
> Echo or mirror seeking of itself,
> And makes a toy of Thought . . .

The house where I lived was large and perched up on a little hill. There was a Tudor gate-house, and you looked through the double arches to a wooden stairway, rather like those steps I was afterwards to be familiar with in dug-outs. The stairway was a steep short-cut to the house. From the house along the ridge of the hill ran an avenue of silver firs. One evening I walked along the moss-grown path of the avenue towards a plantation, to which a stile gave entrance. As I was nearing the stile I heard the most entrancing sound I have ever heard—the long low note of a nightingale. It was a darkling wood and the air was still and the note stood out for me to hear. My father could make a word stand out when he was reading. It stood out with a new meaning. So this note. But what the meaning was I cannot say. Meaning? Must everything have a meaning? Meaning 'must have a stop.' I stood stock-still and heard this note and then the merry tumbled rhapsody of his song. And my swift afterthought was, ' I wish my father could hear it.'

My father loved sitting up late and talking. My elder brother and I kept him company. In the small hours of the morning he would say, ' Well, you two, we should never go to bed at all, unless I made a move.' How unwilling he was to make that move!

My next appointment was at a school in Kent. I remember one or two of my occupations or pre-occupations. I played games hard—harder than before or since. I became a glutton for games. One afternoon, after I had finished playing ' Soccer ' for the school, the captain of a London ' Rugger ' team,

who had borrowed our ground for a match with the
Town, asked me to play for him, as he was short of
a three-quarter. I donned an unfamiliar jersey and
played.

I was reading Aeschylus's *Agamemnon*. I trans-
lated the choruses into English verse and sent them
to my father.

Some miles from the town was a wood. Whenever
I could I walked there. ' There is a quiet spirit
in these woods.' I suppose the spirit was quiet, but
beneath the quietness I felt intensely alive. I cannot
say what quality the life had—primeval perhaps, as
if I were waking in the dawn of time and finding
companionship in trees or in men as trees walking,
an incommunicable blessing, a welding and unifying
passion, pure as the dawn itself. I went back into
the town and found all things new.

I watched *Britannia* and first or second *Valkyrie*
racing in the river. An old sailor was near me, and,
as the Prince's yacht sailed by, he said, ' There goes
the art of man.' In the woods it was the art of God,
and this lovely white thing was like one of God's
birds, and yet it was the art of man also. There was
a reconciliation.

This sense of reconciliation stood me in stead when
my mother summoned me home. My father had
come to the ' last lap,' as he called it. My mother
and I took turns in nursing him. She told me that
when my turn was over and she relieved me I fell
asleep in a moment. My father was full of anxiety
about the future of his business, but his anxiety gave
place to an incoherent joy. In his half-conscious

state he watched a pair of house-martins who had built under the eaves. He could not see the nest, but he knew where the nest was, and his glee at the movements of the male bird was like a child's.

After he died, my mother lost the memory of three weeks and thought my father was still alive and calling her. The attack could not have lasted long, because, when I went to the station to meet my elder brother, she was fit to be left.

Poor brother! He had hurried back from Paris. I was for sending for him before and only refrained on my mother's strict injunction: ' Dad did not wish him to be interrupted in his studies.' The station-meeting was painful. He was terribly vexed at not being summoned in time as well as moved by the sense of loss. He was more moved than I was. I had the comforting feeling of reconciliation. The woods and the yacht had helped me.

I returned to my work. Somehow the place had lost its savour or I had lost my salt, and when I was offered a mastership at a smaller school in the neighbourhood of my old haunts I accepted it. Quite unexpectedly, in the course of my first term, I had a chance to go to Canada, and the dear man whom I served released me, and I found myself travelling to Liverpool with my mother. She was one of the world's heroines. Time would fail me to tell of her patience and fortitude. I am afraid I did not appreciate her as I ought to have done. A young uncle taught me long afterwards of her charm and beauty and spontaneous gaiety as a young woman. Her later life was full of sorrows and of cares. She lived to see a younger daughter of mine. I shall not forget the love in her face when she took this unique little person in her arms. Sylvia my daughter's name was. ' Who is Sylvia? ' I cannot say. She moves about in worlds unrealised by me. She is a child still, I feel sure. Hers is an unknown mode of being, nevertheless, and only laughing echoes float down upon the breeze of time.

I knew a boy in Canada. Of course, he was one of many boys. But now he seems to be the only boy I really knew. His father was a poor Anglican parish-priest on the edge of the continent. He meant to follow in his father's steps. He told me that his father had to be everything to his people, and, therefore, that he himself was going to qualify in medicine first. One of the other prefects said that this boy was ' too good to be true.' I said, ' He is true. He is at least as real as you are, if that is what you mean.'

' That isn't what I mean, sir.'

' Well, what do you mean? '

' I mean that he won't be able to stand shocks. He can't stand our shocks, let alone the shocks that are coming to him.'

' He is just ordinary,' I said. ' He plays games and he does what everybody else does. I ought not to be discussing him with you. It's bad form.'

He laughed. ' I thought " good form " was one of your pet aversions.'

' All right, go on. Tell me what you mean by shocks.'

This prefect's feeling was ratified by the event. The boy I knew was drowned saving the life of another,

who had dived into a deep pool of the Massawippi
River and struck a sunken log. His fellow-prefect's
feeling was the same then as mine, in a later year,
about Sylvia. I felt that this harsh world was too harsh
for her to be happy in; her interest in everybody was
too passionate for her to keep steady; she was too
vulnerable.

The Canadian woods in the Fall were a blaze of
colour—Autumn tints is too faint a word—and the
snow in Winter and the purple glow upon the
mountains just before the daylight faded were very
impressive and mysterious, but I ought to have
gathered more than I did from these sights. I was
pre-occupied with work, with marriage, with the birth
of a daughter, with a longing to return to England.

But when we returned I was not satisfied. Then I
came in contact with the Society of Friends, and
through them, strangely enough, I was led to offer
myself for Holy Orders in the Church of England,
the fold in which I had been reared. That should
have been a turning point in my life. One forgets.
I was conscious of a deep, secret and growing de-
votion to the Christ, of which I was more than half
ashamed.

We moved about from place to place under the
stress of events and desires, as most people do, though
the stress is not in all cases so imperious as ours was.
Under such a stress I came to a decision in 1915 that
was critical in all our lives.

Looking back over the interval between my ordi-
nation and this critical decision, I find my first and,
for a long time, my only visionary experience. I will

describe it as exactly as possible. I was then vicar
of a pretty parish and, apart from the enormous house
in which we had to live, everything was working
smoothly and easily. The people were responsive,
the church was . . . well, satisfactory. I walked
down to conduct a choir-practice. I had a feeling of
well-being. My heart was lifted up. The serene
Summer evening seemed made for me.

I was early and was first at the church. I thought
I could spend my solitude profitably in prayer. I
knelt down at the altar-rails. Almost instantly I saw
a cross of wood—gnarled, ugly, terrifying. It
swayed in mid-air. I wondered why it swayed. Then
I perceived the figure of a man clinging desperately
to the foot of it. His efforts to hold on were
grotesquely painful. His grasp was by his finger-
tips. His back was towards me. I noticed with a
kind of shame the starting muscles. He was
struggling for dear life, in the imminent danger of
falling away. The cross kept rising, gyrating, and
the man's body rose and gyrated with it. He twisted
and throbbed and his fingers bled. Slowly, slowly,
more and more painfully he rose, until I could see
his agonised legs and then his feet and then
the whole man clear. And at the moment when the
cross rose out of sight he twirled round and I recog-
nized his face as my own.

This vision was an objective vision, a ' bodily
sight,' perceived by some faculty of the mind. I was
fully awake. Throughout the very short time occupied
by the vision I was conscious of the ticking of the
vestry-clock, the vestry forming part of the church

screened only by a curtain. As I knelt down at the altar-rails I was chagrined to hear footsteps in the church, and the new-comer had not advanced more than a few paces when the vision was over. In fact, I walked some little distance down the middle aisle to greet him. He said, ' I hope I did not interrupt you.' I said, ' No, it was over.' ' Oh ! ' he said. I meant to tell him my experience, but I suddenly decided not to do so. I went on with the rehearsal as usual.

I can hardly believe that this happened thirty years ago.

Two friendships made a difference—one at this time, and the other, two or three years later. As both these friends have died, I can speak more freely of them. The first was a good scholar, Arthur Clarke, who was then vicar of Cheddar. I was asked to give some theological lectures in his village, and I stayed the night with him each week. I used to ride a bicycle from my pretty parish, over the moor and down the Gorge. My journeys were during the late Autumn and early Winter. Cheddar Gorge is awesome in the gathering gloom of an afternoon when the days are closing in and few people are about and the mighty rocks stoop over you as you pass. Augustus Toplady is said to have written his hymn, ' Rock of Ages, cleft for me,' in the shadow of the Lion Rock, but the cleft is the whole gorge. It is as if the hill, struck by a giant axe, had gaped open under the blow and the axe had pierced through to the foundation, the top of the gash being the axe-head and the road the edge of the blade. The gorge

itself prompted in me no thought of the Refuge which
is Christ. Yet my first experience of riding there has
left an impression of beauty. For as I was nearing
the Lion Rock I heard a voice singing, a woman's
voice, and the sound went echoing round and seemed
to fill the lonely place with the life it lacked. The
road was slippery and I was riding with caution, and
it was a few moments before I caught up with the
woman. She was on horseback returning from
hunting and was walking her horse and sitting care-
lessly. She straightened up and ceased singing as
I passed. I saw her again in the evening and Clarke
introduced me to her after the lecture, but I was too
shy to tell her of the gift that came through her—gift
of hearts' ease in the sound of song, healing all gloom
and loneliness.

The third time I stayed with him, Arthur and I
talked about a book I was writing. He looked at me
with a kind of envy. He said, ' I devitalised myself
getting a Fellowship.' Then, as if to disprove his
words he began to soliloquise—I can only call it that.
It was about analogies, suggested by an analogy I had
made in the course of my lecture. I sat rapt, as I had
done when my father read the *Ancient Mariner*.
Arthur's words flowed from him without pause or
hint of effort. He seemed a channel for ideas. He
was himself, of course—characteristically himself—
a brown-bearded man of extreme delicacy of face, with
a steep brow and a low-pitched thin voice, a man as
full of the milk of human kindness as he was of
learning; he was also, I felt, not himself, but the
mouthpiece of some tutelary spirit.

Later in the evening he made a quotation. ' You remember what the Pope says about Guido :

> I stood at Naples once, a night so dark . . .'

The passage is familiar enough to me now and to most of my possible readers, but then it was new. I had read Browning : *Pippa Passes, Men and Women, Christmas Eve and Easter Day, Karshish* . . . but I had shirked *The Ring and the Book*.

The effect of the quotation was for me momentous. The next morning I sent for a copy of *The Ring and the Book*, and when it came I spent three days reading it through. It was an unforgettable experience. Browning's discovery of the Old Yellow Book was almost personal to me. ' A Hand always above my shoulder.' [1] So that was how he lived. And his invocation of Elizabeth after she had died,

> —so blessing back
> In those thy realms of help, that heaven thy home,
> Some whiteness which, I judge, thy face makes proud,
> Some wanness where, I think, thy foot may fall. [2]

The tutelary spirit might be such as Elizabeth. And Pompilia. She was Elizabeth, too. She was the Pompilia of the old story, just as Robert found her ; she was also Elizabeth. Caponsacchi was Caponsacchi ; he was also Robert, who had rescued his bird from the cage. The relegated priest's longing for the life—now impossible—of a poor private man with her to help him :

> I do but play with an imagined life
> Of who, unfettered by a vow, unblessed
> By the higher call,—since you will have it so,—
> Leads it companioned by the woman there.
> To live, and see her learn, and learn by her . . .[3]

[1] *The Ring and the Book*, I, 40. [2] *Ibid.*, 1413-1416. [3] *Ibid.*, VI, 2081.

was Robert's own cry for the renewal of the perfect companionship he had known. The Pope's praise of Pompilia was essentially Robert's praise of Elizabeth. Pompilia's praise of Caponsacchi was not essentially different from Elizabeth's praise of, or, rather, gratitude for, Robert in *Sonnets from the Portuguese*. Guido? Guido in the poem was not the Guido of the portrait. Examine ' Ritratto del' infelice Guido Franceschini.' Guido in the poem has an intellect as quick and sharp as Browning's and his casuistical penetration. Did Browning distrust his intellect? Did he rely more and more upon the Hand always above his shoulder? Did he believe in intuition (Clarke had hinted at this), the whisper?—

> . . . One less true than thou
> To touch, i'the past, less practised in the right,
> Approved less far in all docility
> To all instruction,—how had such an one
> Made scruple ' Is this motion a decree? '
> It was authentic to the experienced ear
> O' the good and faithful servant.[1]

I felt that the poet was declaring his own secret as well as Pompilia's. I felt also that there were sublime passages of poetry which could only have ' come ' direct. They sounded as spontaneous as the stories of the Gospel : ' Who is my neighbour? And Jesus answering said . . . .'

The second friendship began on this wise. We had left the pretty parish, driven out by the big house, and I had reverted to a curacy in a country-town, of which one merit was that we could easily get out of it into the delightful neighbourhood of my wife's

[1] *The Ring and the Book*, X, 1086. The *askesis* for the intuition.

early sojourn. One Sunday, after Evensong, a tallish, rather gaunt man with a face like Savonarola, only less heavy, walked into the vestry and said, ' My name's Sharp. I hoped I should find you " up " this evening.' By ' up ' he meant ' in the pulpit.' I knew instantly that nothing would ever stop him.

' How splendid of you to come! '

' A little book of yours hit me in the eye.'

I did not ask him which little book. I wondered, even then, of what use I could be to him, because it was certain that he wanted me to be of use.

I had discussed with Clarke an interpretation of the Unjust Steward, and I had suggested that the Steward was praised for his single-mindedness, and Clarke had quoted *The Statue and the Bust*. Whatever be the fate of the irresolute, the men and women of divided aims,

> Only they see not God, I know,
>   Nor all that chivalry of His,
> The soldier-saints who, row on row,
>   Burn upward each to his point of bliss—
> Since the end of life being manifest,
>   He had burned his way through the world to this.

Cecil Sharp was that single-minded man who would burn his way through the world. He was in the grip of a great mission—not, like the Steward's, a wholly selfish mission—but, like the Steward, he was going to make friends to himself for the furtherance of his mission. During our twenty years' friendship we often talked of other things than Folk Songs and, later, Folk Dances and Folk Plays, but not for long. He wrote me letters, in which he mentioned other things, but Folk Music and his efforts to disseminate

Folk Music occupied the greater space. I have mentioned elsewhere [1] his recognition of the highest qualities of our nature in the humblest peasants, and I have called this his true greatness, but the quality for which he has earned the praise of men was his single-mindedness.

A woman who used to work in my house told me that she ' never 'ad a misword with her 'usband.' I asked her what she meant precisely by never having a misword. She said, ' Theein' and thouin' an' cursin' an' swearin'—that's what I do mean.' Cecil Sharp and I never had a misword. Not only did we *not* ' thee and thou,' but there was not the slightest sign of any the slightest rift in our friendship from first to last. I admired him beyond expression, partly, I suppose, because he possessed this quality of single-mindedness, which I so conspicuously lacked. Sometimes I loved him, but my feeling of love was not due to his single-mindedness. I perceived that the pursuit of a mission may make a man ruthless. I think I loved him for his unexpected humilities.

Cecil Sharp did a great work for the nation, because at the age of forty he realised that he was not a great musician and became single-minded in the pursuit of a high aim. He said to me once that his work was hack-work. The generally useful work of the world is hack-work, often literally hack-work, like coal-getting. Cecil Sharp gave up composing music, because he felt that his music had to be composed; that his music was hack-work when it ought to be something else, and he was humble enough to apply

[1] See *London Mercury*, April 1928.

his mighty power of industry and his musical craftsmanship to collecting music that had not been ' composed.' He recognised, that is to say, that music which is more than musical noises must be intuitive—it must ' come ' as ' naturally ' as the quiet tune of the hidden brook—and that the best craftsmanship is useless unless it does come.

When he contended for the ' communal origin ' of folk-music, he meant that folk-song was the intuitive product of simple people. Some tale—it may be of far-off forgotten things like the doings of Lord Rendal's sweetheart [1]—floats into the mind of a labourer when he is ' out to plough ' and a fragment of a tune comes with it. He may have his own sense of form or the tale may be kept going until it reaches a man who has, and the song becomes 'fixed ' as his song. It is passed on, probably to his son, and then to his son's son, until finally it is heard by the ' hackwork ' musician, who sends it back to the elementary schools and other places. It was Cecil Sharp's most earnest desire that the songs he had gathered from the poor should be restored to the children of the poor, though, as a matter of fact, the first persons to whom he taught the songs were members of the Royal Family and boys at a preparatory school for Eton.

The simple person I loved best of Cecil Sharp's singers was John Short of Watchet, who died in 1933 at the age of 95. I met him first in the month before the War. Cecil Sharp was staying with us at my

---

[1] My father used to hum the refrain of this song, but that was all he remembered.

country vicarage-house (I had moved again reluc-
tantly) in the neighbourhood of Watchet, and during
three successive days John Short sang 63 sea-
shanties, 13 of which had not before been noted in
any version. Apart from his singing, John Short
taught me many things.

In August 1914 I was in Cambridge, and I gave a
lecture on ' Mysticism in Present-Day Poetry.' I
remember remarking with some unction that when-
ever I read a book on Mysticism I knew what was
coming. I quoted various definitions of Mysticism
and expressed dissatisfaction with them all. I con-
cluded that it passed the wit of man to say what
Mysticism is. As I could not define Mysticism or
say what is meant by a ' mystic,' it was an illogical
proceeding to maintain that any poet was a mystic,
except on the understanding that we all knew what
was implied by Mysticism, even though we were not
able to define it.

II

In September 1915 I was in France serving as a
Chaplain. My eldest son, aged 18, came out in
December. His mother saw him off. She and her
sister had seen me off. I spent a few weeks at a
Base Camp and then went up the Line.

Nothing of relevance happened to me until the
First Battle of the Somme. One day I was wander-
ing back to the place of the ' heavies ' when I saw a
major of artillery whose walk I recognised vaguely.
He accosted me with ' Hallo, sir,' and, looking more

closely, I knew him. He was an old pupil of mine. I walked with him to his battery and we had a scratch meal together. He said he was enjoying every moment and told me that I was ' taking this war too seriously.'

' Isn't it serious? '

' Yes, of course, but I don't believe in taking seriously anything for which you are not responsible. I remember how you used to laugh. One of the things at school I remember best. You told me that " if I did that again I should be led out to instant execution." We both laughed then, but you laughed more than I did.'

I had not looked upon myself as a laughing person, and he ' remembered that best.'

' Who led you to that belief? '

' What belief? '

' In not taking seriously anything for which you are not responsible.'

' You did.'

' I am sure I never said so.'

' Oh, no! But I learned it from you all the same.'

He learned it from me. The nett result of my influence on him was something I had not thought of —a belief or conviction that I felt sure I did not hold. How is anyone taught anything? The imparting of information, the instruction in technique—these are temporary matters; the communication of beliefs is different. And here, before me, stood a man whom I had known as a boy, and the belief that governed him was due to me, and it was a belief that I should have denied for myself. The effect of the belief was to enable him to enjoy his job. It was more : he showed himself as one of the most alert, conscientious and fearless of men. The very morning of our meeting he had returned from performing a task which earned him the Military Cross. And, if you please, the fact that I had laughed with him at school had led to this belief of his.

I arranged with him to take a service for his men after the ' push ' (July 13th, 1916). I was to go to Marlborough Copse on the following Sunday morning. I duly left the trench, where I lived for the moment, at 8 a.m. on the day fixed, and after many adventures I came back to the trench at 2.30 p.m., without finding him. As a matter of fact, his battery did not move to Marlborough Copse. The push, though successful, was not successful enough.

This man's Christian name was Cecil. He fell before the year was out. I had a letter which reached me after he had fallen. There had been many casualties in his unit, and he indicated that he was very weary. I knew somehow that he would die, not having heard when I received the letter that the time of his warfare was actually over and his release had come.

Another release was my son's. But before that happened—and, indeed, my son fell before Cecil, though his death was not confirmed officially until long afterwards—an experience of a crucial kind had befallen me, and it is only now that I perceive how crucial and necessary it was.

I hardly know how to speak of my part in these matters, without appearing to think that my part was important. I was involved, as a non-combatant, in these scenes of death and destruction, of ruin and waste : they were altogether beyond my comprehension, and I do not pretend to know in the least what was taking place from the point of view of God's whole economy. That goes without saying. It should go without saying also that I do not regard any of the events that touched me personally as having only to do with me or principally to do with me. For example, Cecil's death concerned his wife much more deeply than it concerned me, even if it did concern me deeply. My own son's death concerned me very deeply, but I was always conscious that it might concern his mother more and, perhaps, the two sisters who were nearest to him in age. The strangers or comparative strangers, whom I saw die, were, I knew, linked on to their own people at home. After they had died, those people were thinking of them and contriving for them and writing to them in the belief that they were living—I mean, in the interval between the event of death and the announcement of the event. How the event affected me was, I knew, of quite infinitesimal moment in the sum of things. Yet I was being slowly forced into the belief that God has an individual interest in and a delicate care for human beings, as if they were His children. An event that touched me personally was meant to touch me personally. It did not happen for my sake, and yet ' for my sake ' does express something of its meaning. I hear the remark, ' How insolent ! ' I hear myself make the remark. What is man that Thou art mindful of him ? What is one man among all the millions of men ? He is a bit of stellar matter gone cold by accident. He is nothing : not to be accounted of. And yet I have felt myself driven out of this immensity and admonished as a son is admonished by his father.

When I speak, therefore, of an event as having provided me with an experience, I do not imply that the event happened *in order to* provide me with an experience—that would not only be an extreme example of ὕβρις but absurdly grotesque and even insane—but I do imply that in the economy of God the individual is minutely arranged for, and it is possible that these minute arrangements connected with events of manifold significances are the only means by which some individuals may be convinced of truths and, ultimately, of the Truth.

The place was ' Y Wood,' a name given by someone to the top of a ravine that ran down from the Peronne road to the Somme river. The time was an evening in early Autumn, following a period of heavy bombardment by the enemy, when a few ' strays ' only were coming over. I saw one of these strays strike a shallow dug-out, about a hundred yards away from me. I made my way as quickly as possible to the place, with the M.O. hard behind me. When we came to the dug-out we found a man grievously wounded in the entrance and, for the rest, the only sign of humanity was one grey face. The mess-servants of one of our batteries had been playing cards in this dug-out, but we had to call the roll to discover who were killed. At the moment of looking in, like a flash of lightning came the words : ' Now you *know* that there is a Resurrection of the Dead.' Yes, I did know.

My last meeting with my son occurred before this experience. I had seen him twice in France during the previous Winter, and I had spent part of a ' leave ' with him at home in the Spring. On this occasion I found him with difficulty, though he was ' in rest ' not far from us. He told me of a friend of his who had been killed by a ' pip-squeak ' in the face. He made no mention at all of going home.

I invited him to our Mess and ' Joe ' and ' Wu ' and ' Peckham ' made him welcome, and I think it was ' Max ' who dubbed him ' Padre Mark II.' Their welcome moved him inexpressibly. I can see him now crumbling his bread in his agitation, with tears starting to his eyes. Somehow, though I know not how, the sight of him so moved made me believe in the life of the world to come.

But he had something to say of the life that now is. I had gone up to his billet to ask him to dine with us again. He said, ' I can't. I can't.' We walked together to the Albert-Amiens road. He saw some shells falling in Albert, and he remembered casualties to his own platoon while they were having tea in one of the cellars of that place. He said, ' I don't mind shells in the way of business. But when you are having tea ! '

We spoke of a copy of Shakespeare that a lady in Exeter had sent him. He said, ' I have been reading it. The tragedy is a mistake. There is no tragedy in life.' I have thought of this saying a thousand times. It was an intuitive saying. He said it half to himself. He did not defend it or explain it, and I made no comment. If the reader will picture a fair-haired, blue-eyed, tallish youth of eighteen, looking out, as Ham Peggotty looked out to sea ' with the silence of suspended breath behind him,' he will have some feeling of what was happening on the Albert-Amiens Road.

That, as I have said, was our last meeting. We parted there, and, though I turned and watched him walking away until he waś out of sight, he did not turn or make any gesture of farewell.

He went into action two days before we moved to Y Wood, and during ten days of our three weeks' sojourn there I received no Field Post-card from him. We were then ordered North, and we marched at the rate of fifteen to twenty miles a day to Nœux-les-Mines. In Nœux-les-Mines I had a letter : his battalion was still on the Somme in the neighbourhood of High Wood (Bois des Fourreaux)—at least, I guessed so.

During the Somme Battle our guns had been massed for attack. It was possible for me to visit all the batteries in a short space of time. Our next move would be into a ' peace-area ' and the batteries would be much farther apart. On the morning of September 16th I decided to go round to see all the officers and men I could come at, in and about the village. I paid many visits and I asked two or three officers to come to our Mess for tea. As I was walking home along the dirty street I heard a very distinct voice, ' This is the end,' but I paid no heed. The voice came again, ' This is the end,' and a third time. I accepted the words. I began to wonder, ' What end ? ' There seemed to be no question of an end. The end of our rest-period? Too trivial! The end of what? I gave it up. Wait and see.

I was not disturbed, or, I had no consciousness of disturbance. I had forgotten the voice at tea-time. It was a jolly party and I received a belated birthday present, Rupert Brooke's book about his travels. A new M.O. turned up. After tea they all ' pushed off ' except Peckham. He and I were left alone in the room. He was writing a letter. An orderly came in with a ' wire ' for me. The wire was from England, sent by my eldest daughter, and announced that my son was missing. This was the very thing I had striven to avoid. Knowing the chances, I had impressed upon my son that he should give as strict an instruction as possible that ' if anything happened to him ' I should receive from his unit the first notice of it. I was his next-of-kin and was entitled to such notice. I thought I might break the force of the blow for his mother and the others. But his instruction had miscarried.

I took the paper in my hand, and I knew that he had died. In half-an-hour I had been carried to the nearest Clearing-Station—an N.Y.D. case. After a fortnight —part spent at Boulogne—I was sent home.

III

Though I did not return to France, I was given work at home and I was not invalided out of the Army until the following March. Meanwhile I had been brought through a stage of spiritual education. I saw visions. The first was of the Trial and Stoning of Saint Stephen. It was not so swift as the vision of the Gnarled Cross, or, perhaps, it was really more than one Shewing. I cannot be sure. I have described this vision elsewhere. The horror of it was intense, especially of the fox-faced boy who cut the cord that bound Stephen to the low stake, and yet it was a revelation of spiritual beauty, and the strong and necessary insistence seemed to be on forgiveness.

Akin to these visions was a new and startling manner of writing. I felt moved to write. I wrote by injunction and I left off writing by injunction. I took no thought about what I was going to write. The words grew on the paper without any effort of mine, and what the words indicated was often very surprising and always had an effect of life. There were not any pictures in my mind until *after* the words were written, except, of course, when I set out to describe a vision, which recurred as in a mirror. I heard of the spiritualistic theory of ' automatic writing.' ' Automatic ' seemed a false description of my writing. I was not an automaton at all; I remained characteristically myself, and everything I wrote down was on a basis of experience. But there was no labour. The periods during which I was impelled to go on were periods of intense vitality and often so joyous that I lived for them and regretted the word, Stop.

The visions of Christ Himself, that is to say the visions in which He absorbed the attention, as distinct from such a vision as the Stoning of Stephen, when I felt only the thrill that He was there—these visions were the most enthralling moments of my life. ' Indifferent ' and ' ordinary ' are the words I want to use : indifferent, because of a free grace independent of distinction or merit; and ordinary, because of His courteous familiarity. Some theologians—for example, Karl Barth—have contended for His majesty and transcendence, as if they were incompatible with familiarity. But the more He condescended, the more majestic He seemed.

The day came that they told me to go; I was invalided out as unfit for any further service. A few days before, the official telegram had been sent on to me, conveying regrets at my son's death, now officially confirmed. The evidence on which the telegram was based had been known to us for a long time : a corporal scout's report that he had seen him after he was killed—' I knew him well, a tall man and a very young officer.'

My visions failed. They became a memory. I began to be afraid. My fears plagued me. I wanted to be alone and yet I feared to be alone. My irritations had to be restrained and my fears forced down. Physical pain was a relief : it kept me from thinking or whatever the functioning was that had the power to emasculate my inner being. I did not know what to do and there was none to tell me. I was determined of one thing—not to reveal what was happening to my mind. I hoped that I showed no sign of these disturbances. I did not speak of them to any human being.

But, one day, the idea of being ' told ' what to do occurred to me. And I was told. I heard words as distinct as I had heard in Nœux-les-Mines. For the next fourteen or fifteen weeks I listened for instructions and I was given my instructions in clear and unmistakable words.

Sometimes I was told to do things that seemed ill-timed. They were not ill-timed; they were exactly timed. The issue ratified my obedience; it made my obedience seem reasonable.

In the course of my reading, many years after this period, I came upon the phrase, ' prayer of loving attention.' I think I saw it first in the *Ascent of Mount Carmel,* by the Carmelite St. John of the Cross. He insists upon the submission of the will. I wondered if, by any chance, he meant the process that, at first, relieved me from the misery of indecisiveness and afterwards became a strain, or, possibly, what followed on my release from listening. I was undoubtedly ' in a bad way.' It is usually assumed that people in a bad way cannot give any reliable testimony. But I was helped out of the bad way by this process. It had its disadvantages. It tended to divide me from my fellows and to absorb my attention. If I engaged in conversation my answers were slow, because I was waiting for the answers. If, however, the conversation quickened and I forgot myself I answered without listening and felt happier in doing so.

My attention to the words was not consciously loving. I do not remember any feeling of gratitude, but I have not listened to any other words with the same attention or obeyed with the same swiftness and exactitude. My instructions were received at the

moment when I needed them and not before. Any
attempt to anticipate was accompanied by anxiety. It
seemed to be possible to live in the belief that my
actions were ' dictated,' though dictation suggests
that I was irresponsible. As a matter of fact, I knew
that my responsibility was exacted. I was able to
respond and I was at liberty not to respond.

Emotion was completely eliminated. This was a
steel-cold business. I could not experience emotion,
because I was too set upon obedience.

Nor did ' prayer,' as we commonly use it, seem
applicable. I gave up saying prayers. I thought
about other people, but I could not pray for them.
They seemed to be with me in my obedience.

But, perhaps, what John of the Cross meant by the
prayer of loving attention was what followed on my
release from listening. The relief of release was so
great that I jumped for joy—literally. I was in a
railway-station when I was told not to listen any more
and I skipped along the platform like a schoolboy
catching his home-train at the end of term. For I
knew that I might trust my own thoughts, not
because they were my own, but because they would
be aided imperceptibly.

There were two other consequences of my release.
One was that I wrote enormously in the manner I
have tried to indicate. I worked hard at gardening
and poultry-keeping and writing was my effortless
recreation. By a timely gift, I was able to print some
of these writings for private circulation. My name
was not attached to them. I sent one book to a well-
known critic, who happened to be a friend of long

standing, and he thought that I had come into possession of a Coptic MS. and translated it!

The other consequence was a sensibility that I find it hard to describe. Sometimes it was extremely painful and, at other times, strangely glorious. If I heard a distressful cry from a child or a noise of human distress of any kind I was almost appalled. On the other hand, seeing a tree change its appearance in different atmospheres, or a leaf swirling in the road, or a little girl playing with a doll; hearing through the open door of a cottage a woman talking childish nonsense to her infant, or a man greeting his wife when he came home from work—a thousand, commonplace, minute things of this kind set my heart dancing. These things seemed to have a value of eternal gladness. It was more than 'seemed'; I knew they had.

And now I must proceed to my inquiry.

II
VISION

II

VISION

I BEGIN this inquiry with Vision, because Vision was first in my own unusual experiences.

I

Baron Friedrich von Hügel studied ' the mystical element of religion ' in the life of St. Catherine of Genoa and her friends. Her ' conversion ' took place on March 22nd, 1473, and on this day, or on one of the two previous days, she had the following Vision :—' Our Lord, desiring to kindle still more profoundly His love in this soul, appeared to her in spirit with His Cross upon His shoulder dripping with blood, so that the whole house seemed to be all full of the rivulets of that Blood, which she saw to have been all shed because of love alone. And filled with disgust at herself, she exclaimed : " O Love, if it be necessary, I am ready to confess my sins in public." '

On this experience Von Hügel remarks [1] : ' This is, to begin with, her first and last vision (*visione*), which I can find, in the sense of a picture produced

---

[1] *The Mystical Element of Religion*, I, 108, Sec. Ed. 1923 (Dent).

indeed " in the spirit," but yet evidently apprehended with a sense of apparently complete passivity in the perceiving mind and of objectivity as to the perceived thing, and remembered as such throughout her life. For the frequent subsequent " sights " or picturings (*viste*) are avowedly only of the nature of profoundly vivid, purely mental, more or less consciously voluntary and subjective contemplations and intuitions; whilst her only other " visions," those seen during the last stage of her last illness, seem indeed to have been of an even more sensible kind that this *visione,* but they were entirely fitful and left no permanent impression behind them.'

We may venture, then, to call Vision a supernormal mode of apprehension, and the thing apprehended a supernormal phenomenon. It is generally connected in the public mind with an *abnormal* state and sometimes with strange illnesses, and its association with Mysticism has brought Mysticism into discredit. Vision, indeed, has its special dangers, as St. John of the Cross [1] has pointed out. In writing of this phenomenon he begins with a warning [2]: ' There is always ground for fear that visions proceed from the

[1] St. John was John de Yepes, born in Old Castille on June 24th, 1542. He entered the Carmelite Order at the age of 21, and was ordained priest in 1567. He was introduced to St. Teresa de Jésus, who was desirous of forming two houses of reformed friars, the Discalced Carmelites. When St. Teresa became prioress of the Convent of the Incarnation at Avila, St. John was appointed confessor. In 1577 he was taken prisoner by the Calced Carmelites and underwent cruel treatment at Toledo for eight months. He escaped from prison. The opposition of the Calced friars ceased, and the Discalced friars constituted themselves as a special province of the Order. The provincial, Nicholas Doria, treated John of the Cross with great harshness, and he died on December 14, 1591. See *Life of St. John of the Cross* by David Lewis, 1888. *The Spiritual Canticle* was written in prison.

[2] *The Ascent of Mount Carmel,* trans. by David Lewis (1906), p. 104.

devil rather than from God; for the devil has more influence in that which is exterior and corporeal, and can more easily deceive us therein than in what is more interior. And these bodily forms and objects, the more exterior they are, the less do they profit the interior spiritual man, by reason of the great distance and disproportion subsisting between the corporeal and the spiritual . . . . As they are so palpable and so material they excite the senses greatly, and the soul is led to consider them the more important, the more often they are felt.'

Nevertheless St. John experienced Visions, for he speaks [1] very exactly of them : ' Let me now, then, speak of visions of corporeal substances, spiritually presented to the soul after the manner of bodily visions. As the eyes behold bodily things in a natural light, so the understanding, in a light supernaturally derived, beholds interiorly the same natural things, and others such as God wills : the vision, however, is different in kind and form, for spiritual or intellectual visions are much more clear than bodily visions . . . .

' When these visions occur, it is as if a door were opened into a most marvellous light, wherein the soul sees, as men do when the lightning suddenly flashes in a dark night. The lightning makes surrounding objects visible for an instant, and then leaves them in darkness, though the forms of them remain to the fancy. But in the case of the soul the vision is much more perfect; for those things it saw in spirit in that light are so impressed upon it, that whenever God

[1] *Ibid.*, p. 200.

enlightens it again, it beholds them as distinctly as it did at first, precisely as in a mirror, in which we see objects reflected whenever we look upon it. These visions once granted to the soul never afterward leave it altogether; for the forms remain, though they become somewhat indistinct in the course of time.

' The effects of these visions are quietness, enlightenment, joy like glory, sweetness, pureness, love, humility, inclination, or elevation of the mind to God, sometimes more, sometimes less, sometimes more of one, sometimes more of another, according to the disposition of the soul and the will of God.'

Visions are occasional. They occur at a crisis, when the visionary requires some direction, warning, enlightenment or encouragement that he is not ready to receive in any other way. Vision is the clearest and most impressive and arresting of all modes of apprehension. The visionary must be receptive. His other experiences, whether by way of event or conversation or reading or longings or needs (conscious or unconscious) or intense thinking must have prepared him for the vision. Yet he will not have craved for it. Craving for a vision is as disastrous as asking for a sign. The vision will be, in a true sense, involuntary. And if it contains a command to action, the visionary is instantly and naturally and inevitably obedient. The objectivity of the vision seems to ensure that.

Visions are seldom ' open ' They are meant for the persons who receive them. If they are communicable, they are never wholly communicable. Their ' atmosphere ' cannot be communicated, so that what might seem trivial or commonplace in the telling is invested with an indescribable awe or splendour. And the trouble of finding words in which to indicate visions tends to destroy their effect upon the visionary himself. If he speaks, it should only be after a long time.

Many children have visions easily and naturally. They do not distinguish between the visions of the mind and the visions of the eyes. They speak in the same way of both, without any special excitement. A daughter of mine informed me quite calmly that she had seen Jesus, ' and He was leaning up against an apple-tree and He laughed and I asked Him to tell me a story.' This vision remained with her all her life. In a sense, it was her life.

II

The sanest, calmest and sweetest-minded. of all acknowledged cloistered mystics is the English Lady Julian of Norwich. She was an anchoress, and her anchorage was built against the South-eastern wall of a church in the parish of Conisford, near Norwich. She was a strict recluse, but she had two servants to attend her. She did not despise her general health. She seems to have kept the counsels of the *Ancren Riwle* as to the judicious care of the body. In the *Riwle,* anchoresses are exhorted to take care of their diet, to wash regularly, to rest, to avoid idleness and gloom, to read, to sew for Church and poor. ' Ye may be well content with your clothes, be they white, be they black; only see that they be plain, and warm and well-made—skins well tanned; and have as many

as you need. Let your shoes be thick and warm.'
The *Ancren Riwle* is very English!

Lady Julian honoured the body and thought well
of it. She says that Christ waits to minister to us
His gifts of grace ' unto the time that we be waxen
and grown, our soul with our body and our body
with our soul, either of them taking help of the other,
till we be brought unto stature, as nature worketh.'

Her book (*The Revelations of Divine Love*) consists
of ' Shewings ' and her exposition of them during the
space of twenty years. Fifteen of her Shewings were
given on the 8th of May, 1373, between the hours of
4 a.m. and 9 a.m., and the Sixteenth (and final)
Shewing on the night of the 9th May.

She had before this time made certain prayers out
of her longing after more love to God and her trouble
over man's sin. She had come to the age of 30 and
desired a greater consecration. She was sick for
seven days before her Shewings, and then her pain
ceased and she was calm and well. This was on
Sunday morning (May 8th). On the Sunday night
she had a ' horrible Shewing ' in her sleep. None of
her other Shewings came in sleep—she is very careful
to tell us that. She was tempted by this dream to
despair, and on the following night she received
another Shewing (not in sleep) as a conclusion and
confirmation of the other fifteen.

Her first revelation is the most instructive for my
purpose.[1] I conceive that the actual *visione* was

---

[1] My purpose is to indicate as clearly as is possible the nature of
Vision as a mode of apprehension. The reader may be provoked by my
analysis. My answer to him is that Vision is not a confused thing like
a dream, but is sharper in outline than a natural sight and *protected*
from confusion by its brilliancy and swiftness. The square brackets

swift. It passed like the lightning, but the sight of it remained ' as in a mirror,' and while it remained there were presented to her understanding (insight, beholding) two other subsidiary sights and one open example. Her reflections were made *at the time*, but were, of course, written out afterwards. These reflections were a kind of spiritual seeing, and when she came to write were explained according to her power of indicating in words what she had seen— meaning the reflective seeing which is also swift— though, even then, the writing was not adequate to the seeing.

The actual visione : ' Suddenly I saw the red blood trickle down from the Garland hot and freshly and right plenteously, as it were ' in the time of His passion when the Garland of thorns was pressed on His blessed Head who was both God and Man, the same that suffered thus for me. I conceived truly and mightily that it was Himself shewed it me, without any mean (*i.e.*, intermediary).

' And in the same Shewing suddenly the Trinity fulfilled my heart most of joy . . . [And this was shewed in the First and in all : for where Jesus appeareth, the blessed Trinity is understood, as to my sight].

' And I said : Benedicite Domine ! [This I said for reverence in my meaning, with mighty voice . . .

([ ]) indicate the reflection, the spiritual seeing. The asterisks (*) indicate the continuance ' as in a mirror ' of the actual *visione*. The word formed to her understanding is indicated by the *italics* of the subsidiaries. See also the Second Shewing at the outset. I must leave the reader who is interested in Lady Julian's teaching to read the whole of the First Shewing (at any rate) in Grace Warrack's version of the B.M. MS.

Through this sight of the blessed Passion, with the
Godhead that I saw in my understanding, I knew well
that *It* was strength enough for me, yea, and for all
creatures living, against all the fiends of hell and
ghostly temptations].

First subsidiary shewing : ' In this He brought our
blessed Lady to my understanding.   I saw her
ghostly, in bodily weakness : a simple maid and a
meek, young of age and little waxen above a child,
in the stature that she was when she conceived. [Also
God shewed in part the wisdom and truth of her
soul . . .]

[' In this same time our Lord shewed me a spiritual
sight of His homely loving.

' I saw that He is to us everything that is good and
comfortable for us : He is our clothing that for love
wrappeth us, claspeth us, and all encloseth us for
tender love, that He may never leave us; being to us
all-thing that is good as to mine understanding.]

Second subsidiary shewing : ' Also in this He
shewed me a little thing, the quantity of an hazel
nut, in the palm of my hand; and it was as round as
a ball.   I looked thereupon with the eye of my under-
standing and thought : What may this be?   And it
was answered generally thus : *It is all that is made*. I
marvelled how it might last, for methought it might
suddenly have fallen to naught for very littleness.
And I was answered in my understanding : *It lasteth,
and ever shall for that God loveth it*.   And so All-
thing hath the being through the love of God.

[In this Little Thing I saw three properties.   The
first is that God made it, the second is that God loveth

it, the third, that God keepeth it. But what is to me
verily the Maker, the Keeper and the Lover,—I
cannot tell . . .] . . .

   * ' In all the time that He shewed this that I have
now told in spiritual sight, I saw the bodily sight
lasting of the plenteous bleeding of the Head . . .

   ' This Shewing was quick and life-like, horrifying
and dreadful, sweet and lovely. And of all the sight
it was most comfort to me that our God and Lord
that is so reverend and dreadful, is so homely and
courteous; and this most fulfilled me with comfort
and assuredness of soul.

   ' And to the understanding of this He shewed me
this open example.

   Subsidiary open example : ' It is the most worship
that a solemn King or a great Lord may do a poor
servant if he will be homely with him, and specially
if he sheweth it himself, of a full true meaning, and
with a glad cheer, both privately and in company.
Then thinketh this poor creature thus : *And what
might this noble Lord do of more worship and joy to
me than to shew me that am so simple this marvellous
homeliness? Soothly, it is more joy and puissance
to me than if he gave me great gifts and were himself
strange in manner.*

   [' This bodily example was shewed so highly that
man's heart might be ravished and almost forgetting
itself for joy of the great homeliness . . .]

   * ' And as long as I saw this sight of the plenteous
bleeding of the Head I might never cease from these
words : Benedicite Domine ! . . . .

   ' All this was shewed me by three ways : that is to

say, by bodily sight, and by the word formed in my understanding, and by spiritual sight. But the spiritual sight I cannot nor may not shew it as openly as I would. But I trust in our Lord God Almighty that He shall of His goodness and for your love, make you to take it more spiritually and sweetly than I can or may tell it.' [1]

III

Shakespeare was contemporary with St. John of the Cross. He puts into the mouth of Hamlet a warning about Vision similar to that of the Spanish saint :

> The spirit that I have seen
> May be the devil; and the devil hath power
> To assume a pleasing shape; yea, and perhaps
> Out of my weakness and my melancholy,
> As he is very potent with such spirits,[2]
> Haunts me to damn me . . .

There is more than this. Hamlet speaks calmly and, we might almost say, trustfully of his ' mind's eye ' pictures (*viste*) but the *visione* makes night hideous and shakes his disposition horridly. The Ghost's urgent injunction is to treat his mother gently. So far from taking heed to this injunction he is engaged in a merciless exposure of his mother when the Ghost comes again, and after his departure,

[1] The quotations are from *The Revelations of Divine Love*, ed. by Grace Warrack (Methuen) 1901. There are other sources—a shorter version, ed. by the Rev. D. Harford, with the title, *Comfortable Words for Christ's Lovers* (1911) and *Dame Julian*, ed. Dom Hudleston. A good account of Lady Julian's teaching—inherent in her Shewings—will be found in *The English Mystics* by Dom David Knowles (1927). There is reason to believe that Julian was a Benedictine, and her church, St. Julian's in Norwich.

[2] *i.e.*, with weak and melancholy persons.

the 'gentle and loving prince' continues his harsh treatment and behaves at his beastliest.

Between the passage already quoted and Hamlet's meeting with Ophelia is the soliloquy, 'To be or not to be . . .' In this he speaks of

> The undiscover'd country from whose bourn
> No traveller returns . . .

the country that lies beyond death, as if the return of his father's spirit were no return at all. And in his next talk with Horatio—the one man who knows —he speaks of the possibility that his imaginations may be as foul as Vulcan's stithy and the Ghost a damned Ghost.

He indulges in much wild talk after the 'success' of the play and says he will take the Ghost's word for a thousand pound, but it is the play that he relies on for proof of the king's deepest villainy. In his previous talk with Rosencrantz and Guildenstern he has spoken (in prose of a beauty unsurpassed) of the effect of what has happened to him. His apprehension of the joy and excellence and splendour of life is an outward recognition; there is nothing in him to respond to it. He knows without feeling. All he can feel is its barrenness, pestilency, transience.[1]

He does not take the Ghost's word for his father's

---

[1] It is worth noticing that, after Hamlet has praised the 'reason' and 'faculty' of man and his 'form and moving,' he speaks of spiritual qualities: 'in action how like an angel! in apprehension how like a god!' He can act like an angel because of his divine apprehension and this action and this apprehension, above all, make him the beauty of the world and the paragon of animals. The sequence of praise is remarkable. Man is the paragon of animals, because he is (in Aristotle's phrase) a 'contemplative animal,' and for contemplation he can use this divine gift of intuition. Perhaps it may be concluded that Shakespeare, like many highly intuitive persons, distrusted Vision.

present condition. When he comes upon Claudius praying, he hesitates because he *is* praying and his own father was taken grossly,

> And how his audit stands who knows save heaven?
> But in our circumstance and course of thought
> 'Tis heavy with him . . .

He makes the ground of his opinion, not the Ghost's word, but the common acceptance of the value of prayer, of repentance and confession and consequent forgiveness. The initial doubt, ' Thou comest in such a questionable shape,' has become settled.

The last reference to his ' revenge ' is not really to his revenge at all (Act V, Sc. ii). To kill Claudius has become a matter of conscience. He is speaking to Horatio and makes no mention of the Ghost or of his determination to kill Claudius as the acting of his ' dread command.' In fact, the chief reason for killing Claudius is to stop any further evil he may do.

In his dying, Hamlet is not preoccupied with anything at all in the life beyond death. The *visione* has taught him nothing that he believes or trusts about that life. Rather, the effect has been to make him sceptical. He is anxious that Horatio should clear his reputation among his own people and also that his kingdom should be governed well. All he really knows or cares about is what happens here. ' The rest is silence.'

Another poet who warns us of the danger of vision is Robert Browning. There was a visionary period in his own life—probably very short—and he has written a poem, *Christmas Eve,* which I propose to examine, because it is the clearest description of a

' Shewing ' in English poetry. His warning comes, therefore, with the greater force. His own experience of Vision led to a reiterated emphasis on the entire suitability of ordinary experiences for ' carrying on.' He held that Vision or even the certainty of the super-natural which objective vision brings may unbalance us and render us unfit for the life we have to live. In the *Epistle of Karshish* he gives account of one who has had an unusual spiritual experience. Lazarus died and saw life ' from the other side.' Elizabeth Barrett Browning wrote (Dec. 6, 1855): ' The way in which Lazarus is described as living his life after his acquaintance with the life beyond death strikes me as entirely sublime.'

The life itself has elements of sublimity. The man's indignation at carelessness and sin—an indignation promptly curbed—was like the wrath of God. He also caught prodigious import, whole results, in some trifling fact.

But St. Augustine's prayer [1] is that we may see in little things the indications of things both small and great. Lazarus perceived the great and *not* the small. The passing of a mule with gourds is all one with the massing of prodigious armaments to besiege his city. He has lost his sense of proportion. He is unbalanced, perplext with impulses, sudden to start off crosswise. There is a vast distracting orb of glory on either side of the meagre thread of life to which he holds on. He has to lead this earthly life, though he is conscious of the spiritual life which he must not enter yet. He proclaims what is right and wrong *across* this black

[1] *Confessions,* Bk. XI, Ch. xxiii, 1.

thread through the blaze and not along it.   His
heart and brain move there, his feet stay here.

Yet the effect of Lazarus on Karshish is profound.
Lazarus almost convinces Karshish of Christ :

> The very God! Think, Abib, dost thou think?

That is to say, Browning like John of the Cross
knew the value of visions.   In fact, it was the world
of difference between ' vulgar external appearances ' [1]
and the involuntary Shewings—rarely given and
answering to the visionary's spiritual needs—as well
as the feared effect on Elizabeth's delicate organism
that made him impatient of Spiritualism.

IV

§ i. Browning's ' Christmas Eve '

To speak, first, of the manner of this poem :
Browning writes for the most part in octo-syllabic
rhyming verses, and the style of the opening is
grotesque, even flippant.   He visualises intensely the
scene and the people, but the emphasis is upon the
sordidness of the place and the outward repulsiveness
of the men and women and children he encountered.
Picture Lady Julian sitting up in her bed and
beginning by telling us that the room was low and
not very clean ; that she could hear a rat scuttling
about ; that her maidens near by were fast asleep with
their mouths open and in the dim light of her one little
lamp she noticed the ugliness of their ungainly forms

[1] Letter to Miss Isa Blagden, December 19th, 1864 (quoted in my
Browning and the XXth Century, p. 15.)

and lined and stupid faces; that her soul revolted against the place and them. And that she describes it all in a jingle of contemptuous phrases; and you have some parallel to Browning's approach to the holy and awful vision he is preparing to tell us.

A critic might say that he wished to ' throw up ' the vision by contrast with what preceded it and accordingly makes the contrast as violent as possible. I think his manner is exactly suited to the circumstances and character of the vision. The vision was involuntary, sudden, unexpected. It came with the effect of complete surprise. And, therefore, in writing about it, he is determined to show us as exactly as he can the circumstances in which the vision was received, the events and contacts that went before it and the reaction of his own mind to those events and contacts. And he chooses his octo-syllabic line, his grotesque manner of description, his odd and laughable rhymes and comparisons because they combine to indicate his state of mind. He is, one might say, terribly anxious not to mislead his readers; and in his anxiety he probably over-emphasises the sordidness and disgustingness of the preliminary happenings. But even if there is over-emphasis he succeeds in conveying to us the involuntariness of the Vision.

The elaboration of the finished work should not hide from us the swiftness of the Vision and of the Subsidiary Visions and even of the reflections or ' spiritual sights.' These last, in the poem itself, may be the extension into argument of a single word or sentence. A parallel is to be found in a musician's conception of a symphony, taking its rise in a tune or musical phrase and heard as a complete thing in the musician's mind. This may happen in the twinkling of an eye, and the ensuing composition be the work of months. Browning himself tells us of his ' poetic experience ' [1] that came before the writing of *The Ring and the Book*. He made the ' Ring ' out of the ' Book ' *before attempting smithcraft*. He made it on the same day as he found the ' Book,' but the poem engaged his closest attention for more than three years.

(a) *The Visionary tells what happened before the Vision.*

He found himself on Christmas Eve outside a chapel, called Mount Zion, on the edge of a common. He waited in the doorway for full five minutes to escape the driving rain. The porch was of lath and plaster, four feet long by two feet wide (so that he alone blocked up half of it) and divided by a partition from the vast sheep-fold. As he stood there the congregation kept arriving and pushing past him through the creaking door. Some of them came by the main-road, some suddenly emerged through the gaps in the paling, as if they housed in the gravel-pits at the end of the lamp-lit road. But the most of them turned in from a squalid knot of alleys.

> Where the town's bad blood once slept corruptly,
>   Which now the little chapel rallies
> And leads into the day again,—its priestliness
> Lending itself to hide their beastliness

[1] *The Ring and the Book*, I, 457 and ff. For the poet himself, the ' poetic experience ' is everything.

So cleverly (thanks in part to the mason),
And putting so cheery a whitewashed face on
Those neophytes too much in lack of it,
   That, when you cross the common as I did,
   And meet the party thus presided,
' Mount Zion ' with Love-lane at the back of it,
They front you as little disconcerted
As, bound for the hills, her fate averted,
And her wicked people made to mind him,
Lot might have marched with Gomorrah behind him.

Some members of the congregation are ruthlessly described : the fat weary woman, panting and bewildered, downclapping her wreck of whalebones with a mighty report and snorting at the interloper ; the many-tattered little old-faced peaking sister-turned-mother of a sickly babe ; a female something in dingy satins ; a tall yellow man like the Penitent Thief

    With his jaw bound up in a handkerchief ;

a shoemaker's lad with a dirty wizened face and a wet apron wound round his waist like a rope.

They all—except the yellow man, who was blind— seemed to glance at him as at a common prey and resent his intrusion. There was no standing this air of the Grand Inquisitor, and so in the wake of the shoemaker's lad he sent his elbow at the shutting door and found himself in full conventicle.

But there was no standing that, either. The hot smell and the human noises ! Above all, the preaching man's immense stupidity and the divinely flustered state of the flock.

    My gorge rose at the nonsense and stuff of it
    So, saying like Eve when she plucked the apple,
    ' I wanted a taste and now there's enough of it—'

(b) *The oncoming of the Visionary Experience and what he was thinking of at the moment.*

I flung out of the little chapel [1]

He was thinking of the pastor's sermon; of a train journey to Manchester; of his own youth, when the true Church seemed to him to be outside among the immensities, and it was there that he could find evidence of God's love as well as of His power—and even more of His love than His power.

There was calm and storm and then calm again.

(c) *The actual Vision.*

'Twas a moon-rainbow, vast and perfect
From heaven to heaven extending, perfect
As the mother-moon's self, full in face.
It rose, distinctly at the base
  With its seven proper colours chorded,
Which still, in the rising were compressed,
Until at last, they coalesced,
  And supreme the spectral creature lorded
In a triumph of whitest white,—
Above which intervened the night.
But above night too, like only the next,
  The second of a wondrous sequence,
  Reaching in rare and rarer frequence,
Till the heaven of heavens were circumflexed,
Another rainbow rose, a mightier,
Fainter, flushier and flightier,—
Rapture dying along its verge,
Oh, whose foot shall I see emerge,
Whose, from the straining topmost dark,
On to the keystone of that arc?

This sight was shown him—one out of a world of men,

[1] He did not leave the chapel except ' in the spirit.' ' Flung out ' is a way of indicating the abruptness of the experience. It caught him in the middle of a thought.

Singled forth, as the chance might hap
To another, if in a thunderclap
Where I heard noise and you saw flame,
Some one man knew God called his name.

He thought he cried out, like Peter, to make three
tents. The rainbow disparted, the ' too-much glory '
streamed out of it and passed to the ground. He
looked up with terror. Christ was there. He could
recognize the hem of his garment, for this rainbow
was His garment. Christ was going away from him.
Christ had been in the Chapel, then? He was
leaving him now for despising His friends. He
appeals to Him, pleads with Him, and suddenly

The whole face turned upon me full.
And I spread myself beneath it,
As when the bleacher spreads, to seethe it
In the cleansing sun, his wool,—
Steeps in the flood of noontide whiteness
Some defiled, discoloured web—
So lay I, saturate with brightness.
And when the flood appeared to ebb,
Lo, I was walking, light and swift,
With my senses settling fast and steadying,
But my body caught up in the whirl and drift
Of the vesture's amplitude, still eddying
On, just before me, still to be followed,
As it carried me after with its motion.[1]

He followed Christ, holding the hem of His gar-
ment, taking it as a sign that Christ allowed him to
worship and follow in his own way, dispensed from
seeking to be influenced by the less immediate ways
which earth adopts.

[1] For ' saturate with brightness ' compare *Ascent of Mount Carmel* (see
p. 43) and Eckhart's *The Soul's Rage* (see p. 120). For the passivity,
see Von Hügel's *Mystical Element of Religion* (see p. 42). For the
motion, compare Newman's *Dream of Gerontius* (see p. 70). Other
parallels may be found in St Paul's vision on the road to Damascus, in
Ramon Lull's repeated vision of Christ, in St Teresa de Jésus and in
Diary of an Old Soul by George MacDonald, Feb. 24.

(d) *Subsidiary Vision: The Visionary crosses the world with Christ and beholds a miraculous Dome of God.*

He sees, without entering, the whole Basilica alive with men :

> I the sinner that speak to you
> Was in Rome this night and stood and knew . . .
>
> . . . .
> Men in the chancel, body, and nave,
> Men on the pillar's architrave,
> Men on the statues, men on the tombs
> With popes and kings in their porphyry wombs,
> All famishing in expectation
> Of the main-altar's consummation.

Christ, as He goes into the Church, abandons a fold of His robe for the Visionary to hold. He ponders the reason of Christ's entering and his own remaining outside. He thinks he finds the reason in Christ's penetration to the truth athwart the lies.

He thinks to enter, but instead, he becomes absorbed in musing on the love of the first Christian days, of the domination of literature and art and music—distortion, perhaps? Or do they here in Rome offer up all their loves united and bound in a bond of faith? Well, there can never be too much love. But intellect also demands its share.

(e) *Subsidiary Vision: The Visionary goes with Christ to a lecture-hall in a German town.*

Once more, he is left outside. He catches glimpses of the assembly through the open door. And not a bad assembly neither! The Professor, an unworldly artist of the intellect begins his Christmas Eve discourse. The Myth of Christ is his subject. Plainly no such life was livable. How then shall we class the phenomena? Shall we say that Christ was or that He was not, or that He both was and was not? It does not really matter so long as we retain the Idea. The myth has a quite respectable meaning for us . . . .

He resolves to bid the Professor adieu, but he realises that Christ is still staying inside the lecture-hall. Why? Because just when our Professor has reduced our Pearl of Price to dust and ashes, and we are looking for him to sweep it to its natural dust-hole, lo, he confesses it to be a pearl after all—not perhaps the pearl we thought it, but still worth prizing. He urges his hearers to venerate the sacred myth and to adore the Man. Well, the professor's attitude is better than ignorance. And as for his audience, pondering the profit of turning holy for their own sakes, well, they can call themselves Christians if they like.

> Go on, you shall no more move my gravity,
> Than, when I see boys ride a cock-horse
> I find it in my heart to embarrass them
> By hinting that their stick's a mock horse,
> And they really carry what they say carries them.

(f) *The Visionary fears he may lose Christ.*

So he resolves on a gentle tolerance. But while his foolish heart is expanding in a lazy glow of bene-volence over the various modes of man's belief the vesture escapes his hand altogether. He is brought back abruptly to his own life . . .

Meantime, I can but testify
God's care for me—no more, can I—
It is but for myself I know [1]; . . .

.   .   .   .   .   .

                              So viewed,
No mere mote's breadth but teems immense
With witnessings of providence:
And woe to me if when I look
Upon that record,[2] the sole book
Unsealed to me, I take no heed
Of any warning that I read!
Have I been sure this Christmas-Eve,
God's own hand did the rainbow [3] weave,
Whereby the truth from heaven slid
Into my soul?—I cannot bid
The world admit he stooped to heal
My soul, as if in a thunder-peal
Where one heard noise, and one saw flame
I only knew he named my name.[4]

Suppose it is the prelude to death—like the calling
of a conscript's name to serve in the battle-line,
summoned to end his life where his life began—
would it not prove worth while then to have held on
to the vesture?

[1] This certainty for self may be compared with St. Catherine of Siena.
She said in a letter to Raimondo da Capua: ' Father, thou canst be
quite certain that no man has ever taught me any rule of spiritual life,
but only my Lord and Master, Jesus Christ, Who either through some
secret impulse sent by Him, or through His speaking to me, has always
taught me what I ought to do.' (Quoted by Piero Misciattelli in *The
Mystics of Siena*, p. 103.)

[2] Meaning, the record of his own experience.

[3] He refers to the rainbow as the actual *visione*—in a sense, the whole
vision. The rainbow persisted throughout. His hold on this ' vesture '
of Christ may be compared to the persistence of the Garland in Lady
Julian's first Shewing. ' Slid into my soul ' is Coleridge's account of the
coming of sleep (*Ancient Mariner*). Through this vision truth slid into
the poet's soul as softly and easily as sleep.

[4] This passage about the calling of his name is repeated with a
significant alteration. Before, ' Some one man knew God called his
name '; now, ' I only knew he named my name.' The naming of his
name was all he knew and conveyed all that was needful for the healing
of his soul.

(g) *The Visionary Experience ends.*

> And I caught
> At the flying robe, and unrepelled
>   Was lapped again in its folds full-fraught
> With warmth and wonder and delight,
> God's mercy being infinite.
> For scarce had the words escaped my tongue,
> When at a passionate bound [1] I sprung,
> Out of the wandering world of rain
> Into the little chapel again.

So ends the visionary experience. He has never left the chapel. He insists on the truth of the Vision :

> For the Vision, that was true, I wist,
> True as that heaven and earth exist.

He also insists, humorously, that the Vision did not occur in sleep. He could hear the preacher all the time and could give a report of what he said. In fact, the Vision had come to its abrupt close before the preacher had concluded his sermon, and the poet took the opportunity of putting down some notes of what he had seen. He tells us that, when a hymn from Whitfield's Collection was given out to be sung to the tune Hepzibah, he ' put up pencil ' and joined Chorus with the others.

The effect [2] of the experience was not only the

---

[1] This ' passionate bound ' into the chapel corresponds to his abrupt ' flinging out.'

[2] One may compare both these effects with those of George Meredith's intuitive experience, described in *A Faith on Trial* (*The Poetical Works of George Meredith*, with some notes by G. M. Trevelyan, 1912, pp. 345-361). It occurred on a May-day morning, when his wife lay dying. He went out alone for one of their familiar walks in the neighbourhood of Boxhill. He passed some children beginning their rounds of May-day games, and he was irritated by their ' metal ding-dong.' He observed everything as he went along, but without any feeling. Reason failed him in his grief; his philosophy was torn to rags. Then, by the old Pilgrim's Way, leading to Canterbury, he caught sight

healing of his soul but the realisation of his fellow-
ship with those he had despised

§ ii

*Richard Rolle's ' My truest treasure sa traitorly was
taken.'*

The work of Richard Rolle has been thoroughly
sifted during the last ten years, mainly by Miss
Frances Comper in England and Miss Allen in
America. When I began to study Old English (then
called Anglo-Saxon) and Middle English, Richard
Rolle's chief writing was said to be *The Prick of
Conscience,* a long poem of 10,000 lines. It has
since been established that this poem is not his work.
But his place in the line of English mystics, as the
forerunner of Walter Hilton of Thurgarton Priory
and Lady Julian of Norwich, is now incontestable.

The exact date of his birth is unknown—probably
1300. The place of his birth was Thornton-le-Dale
in Yorkshire. He was sent to Oxford but ran away
from the University without taking a degree. He
ran home, but very soon afterwards he borrowed some
clothes from his sister, altered them to make them
look like a hermit's dress, and, when his sister cried

---

of a wild cherry-tree in blossom, and his soul was healed and his faith
restored. The white banner of the blossoming wild cherry with its
' victorious rays over death ' taught him not to rely on his intellect alone
but to believe in and trust his intuitions.

On his way home he saw the children again, and they had him in tune
with the hungers of his kind. He gave them their fee, and watched
them hop and skip to the ' next easy shedders of pence.' Why not?

Compare also Claudel's parable of *Animus* (rational knowledge) and
Anima (intuitive or ' mystical ' knowledge—' mystical ' is Bremond's
word) quoted by Henri Bremond in *Prière et Poésie,* p. 112.

out that he was mad, literally ran away from her and home as well. He went for twenty-four miles and found a place with John de Dalton, a friend of his father's, who gave him a separate lodging and enabled him to pursue the life of a contemplative. He withdrew eventually to Hampole, and, though a layman or only in minor orders, became the confessor of the nuns of Yedingham Priory, for one of whom he wrote his *Ego Dormio*. He is thought to have died in the Black Death of 1349.

Richard Rolle has affinities with Blake. Song was necessary to him. He sang his prayers to notes. It was said of him, as Kate Blake said of ' Mr Blake,' that he lived the most of his time in Paradise. And, as in Blake, there are in his lyrics actual repetitions or very close variants of the same line or phrase. Many of these lyrics are incorporated in his prose works, especially *Ego Dormio*, or correspond to passages of his prose.

We are now concerned with one of his lyrics [1] on the theme of Christ's Passion as containing a possible example of Vision. The first stanza speaks of Christ as the poet's truest treasure, of the traitorous taking of Christ, of His binding, of the forsaking of His servants, of His being struck. In the second stanza, Christ is addressed as ' My well of my weel,' hands twisted behind him, pulled out of prison to Pilate, suffering the hurts and knocks of those who led and followed Him, when they shot into His face both slaver and slime. In the third stanza Christ is the

[1] Taken from *The Life of Richard Rolle together with an Edition of his English Lyrics (now for the first time published)* by Frances M. M. Comper (Dent. 1928; reissued 1933), pp. 275, 276, 277.

' hope of his heal,' hied to be hanged, loaded on with the cross and crowned with thorn, His steps goaded, His back nigh to breaking.

The fourth stanza describes the vision :—

> My salve of my sare, sa sorrowful in sight,
> Sa naked and nailed, thy rig on the rood
> Full hideously hanging, they heaved thee on height,
> They let thee stab in the stane; all steeked there
>   that stood.

This is a new element, not to be found in the frescoes or pictures of the tortured Christ with which the poet was familiar. He sees Him naked and nailed, and, as the executioners heave the cross up—the cross being turned round, held anyhow as if there were no body on it—he sees His back. Then the cross is dropped into the hole made ready for it, but the hole was not packed in with earth, so that it might stand firm, but with loose stones, so that it might sway and cause the Crucified more pain. Or, if ' the stane ' be understood of a socket—and a stone socket seems to be unlikely—there would still be a swaying cross. The word ' steeked ' is used of corn bound together (stooks), and suggests the tops waving in the wind.

This direction for the fixing of the cross may have come from Pilate. The Romans considered the uncomplaining endurance of pain godlike, and Pilate, with the implication of Christ's words in his mind, might have imposed this test of His fortitude or supernaturalness. Pilate's history shows him prone to cruelty, not perhaps a sadist, but indifferent to the sufferings he inflicted on others.

It seems impossible that Richard Rolle should have

invented the excessive torture here indicated. He
recorded the scene because he saw it. His next ob-
secration (for obsecration it is) is ' My dearworthy
darling,' as if the sight of such pain moved him as a
mother would be moved seeing her child suffer.

In the following stanza he escapes from the dread-
ful realism of his vision to the conception of the
trouvères and of the *Ancren Riwle* : Christ as a
knight who has fought through his tournament,
lighting down lovingly that his shield may be unlaced
by Mary and her mengey.

The final stanza is a direct prayer :

> My peerless prince so pure, I thee pray
> Thy mind of this mirror thou let me nought miss;
> But wind up my will to wone with thee ay,
> That thou be buried in my breast and bring me
> to bliss.

' Thy mind of this mirror.' To such as Richard
Rolle the crucifixion was the mirror of God's love.
They have been called ' men of one event,' but that
event was not a murder done in Jewry, something to
blacken Pilate's name or curse Iscariot for, it was the
death, the exodus that Christ set Himself to fulfil,
and it was in deep contemplation of it that they
learned to speak of God as Love.[1]

§ iii

John Henry Newman's ' The Dream of Gerontius.'

This poem bears marks of containing the record of
a visionary experience of the author.

[1] Compare St Catherine of Genoa : ' Love, if it be necessary, I will
confess my sins in public,' (see p. 41).

I have hitherto used the word ' Vision ' in its strict first meaning [1] and ' Dream ' for something that happens in sleep. It may be that Newman uses ' Dream ' inexactly, as Shakespeare does in the title, *A Midsummer Night's Dream* or Tennyson in *A Dream of Fair Women*. But he may have used the title with intent to indicate that the experience of the second part of the poem, in which the speaker is not Gerontius but the Soul of Gerontius, is the half-waking experience of an old sick man—himself—and not, as Lady Julian's was, the wide-awake experience of a youngish person who had been ill but was, at the time of the experience, refreshed and well.

I mentioned this theory to my brother, W. A. Brockington. He told me that he was a guest of Sir Edward and Lady Elgar at the time Sir Edward was composing the music of his oratorio, and that the question arose of the proper pronunciation of the name, Gerontius. My brother suggested that the name was derived from γέρων and that, therefore, the G was hard. Cardinal Newman's chaplain was consulted and he confirmed my brother's suggestion.

The experience, then, is of an old man. The experience is of something that is not strictly objective vision. It lies somewhere between the subject of this chapter and the subject of the next. Nothing is seen objectively; words are heard, but the hearing is so vivid that presences are suggested. I am able to give an example from my own experience. I was alone and in pain of body and distress of mind—the distress of mind being partly due, not to the fear of death, but

[1] Shorter Oxford English Dictionary, p. 2362.

to a sense of isolation which I find it hard to describe. Suddenly I heard a voice. And *with* the hearing of the voice—not after it, but actually as the words were formed to my understanding—I had these successive impressions. First, I thought it was a child's voice : it was fresh, spontaneous, gay, with a kind of radiance in it, and suggested a fearless, laughing child. Next, I thought it was a woman's voice : it was tender and compassionate, and suggested a woman engaged in ministering to her lover, who was sick and helpless. And then I knew it for a man's voice : it was strong, robust, inspiriting, and suggested a father calling across a trench to his son. The words were : ' Can't you trust me ? '

I will call Newman's experience Vision, for lack of another word. The experience was very swift. St. Augustine's *quasi coruscatione perstingeris* applies. So far as time is concerned, the interval occupied is negligible. There are indications of the swiftness of this Vision in the poem itself. Soul says to the Angel :

> What lets me now from going to my Lord?

The Angel answers :

> Thou art not let; but with extremest speed
> Art hurrying to the Just and Holy Judge :
> For scarcely art thou disembodied yet.
> Divide a moment, as men measure time,
> Into its million-million-millionth part,
> Yet even less than that the interval
> Since thou didst leave the body; and the priest
> Cried ' Subvenite,' and they fell to prayer;
> Nay, scarcely have they yet begun to pray.
>
> . . . .
> But intervals in their succession
> Are measured by the living thought alone,
> And grow or wane with its intensity.

And, much later in the poem :

> SOUL :   I hear the voices that I left on earth.
>
> ANGEL :   It is the voice of friends around thy bed,
>   Who say the ' Subvenite ' with the priest.

The poet also indicates the condition of the vision-
ary : silence and a sense of deep rest; the feeling that
he was out of the body and yet in the body; a gentle
pressure that tells him he is not self-moving.[1]

The poem opens with an account of a dying man [2]
(Gerontius) : the sense of ruin; the strange innermost
abandonment; his prayers and the prayers of his as-
sistants; his fierce and restless fright; his commenda-
tion of himself and the Proficiscere of the priest.

Then comes the Vision. It is of an Angel whom
the visionary, here called the Soul of Gerontius,
hears. Through the Angel he apprehends the story
of man's life as a contest between the demon dire
that was not of his nature and the Angel-guardian.
The sounds that are the secondaries of the vision are
the sour and uncouth dissonances of unseen demons
and the singing of the choirs of angelicals. The
demons describe themselves as ' chucked down ' by a
tyrannous despot, and mock at saintship and what
qualifies for beatitude. The choirs tell in a five-fold
song the story of Creation and Redemption. Through
the angelical sounds persists the word, ' Praise ' :
' Praise to the Holiest in the height,' as in Lady
Julian's First Shewing persisted *Benedicite Domine*.
The visionary himself seems to be passing through

---

[1] Compare *Christmas Eve*, p. 59.
[2] The music of the oratorio is not congruous.

a Judgment Court into a House of Judgment, and then, by the Sacred Stair, into the Presence Chamber.

The vision is thrilled through, as all Christian vision is, by Jesus. Not only in the hymns and in the pleading of the Angel of the Agony but in the Soul of Gerontius : his longing to see or, at least, hear ' with personal intonation ' his dearest Master; the promise of the sight of Him; his eager spirit darting from the Angel's hold and flying to the feet of Emmanuel.

The song of the Fifth Choir of Angelicals has become a famous hymn. It can hardly be understood without the songs of the other choirs,[1] and the songs taken together supply the theology of God's dealings with man. The Second Choir has a moment of inspiration : God

> In patient length of days
> Elaborated into life
> A people to His praise!

I suggest that Newman made no claim, except the implicit claim of the title and its contents, that this poem was the result or elaboration of objective vision, partly because the experience came when he was not in robust health and partly because he did not wish to dwell upon the origin of his work. His condition as an invalid is described in the first and non-visionary part of the poem, and there may be a veiled reference to it in the last stanza of the second part, for this sounds like the comforting farewell of a friend to one who has passed the crisis of his illness

[1] These stanzas are very unequal. Newman has worked over the visionary experience in the interests of didacticism.

but is feeling the wearisome burden of life and longs for companionship in order to bear it:

> Farewell, but not for ever! brother dear,
> Be brave and patient on thy bed of sorrow;
> Swiftly shall pass thy night of trial here,
> And I will come and wake thee on the morrow.

Visions are meant for the visionary. One wonders what effect this vision had upon the mind of Newman himself. It seems as if he went in terror of death, as another stout Christian, Dr. Samuel Johnson, confessed that *he* did. The language the dying Gerontius uses is not, in my experience of dying persons, characteristic of those who are near to death. They are reconciled to dying—even the young. But it is the language of one who is not mortally ill and only fears that he may be. So that the first part of the *Dream of Gerontius* is true to the experience of Newman but not to the supposed experience of Gerontius, and the vision may have served to reassure him in his fierce and restless fright.

I had written these remarks about the poem *before* making any enquiry into the history of Dr. Newman, afterwards Cardinal. I had not read Wilfred Ward's *Life,* and I had heard nothing of what happened to Newman in 1864—the *Dream of Gerontius* was published in 1865—except that his *Apologia* was published in that year. Ward writes [1] that Newman had a ' vivid apprehension of immediately impending death ' due to some mistaken medical opinion, and on Passion Sunday, 1864, at 7 a.m. he made a note: ' Written in prospect of death.'

[1] Vol. II, p. 76.

With this knowledge I make bold to say that the Vision of the Second Part of the Poem, taken as a whole, may be relied on and may possibly convey to such as need it the same reassurance as it brought to Newman himself. The First Part may not be relied on. It purports to be the experience of a dying man. It is not the experience of a dying man : it is the experience of a man who feared he might be dying. Men may be afraid of death when they are not dying, and in the false prospect of it may feel as Gerontius does.

The Second Part may be accepted as an attempt to set forth Newman's own visionary experience, and the impression is of an encompassing and delicate care working to promote his perfection and his happiness, coupled with the assurance that this individual interest is as wide as the need for it and the possibility of its application. The field of vision is the life of the world to come, but there are not two worlds but one, and dying is an event of man's life. The love that works for man and in man is ever the same.

Each of these poems is a description of a spiritual experience of the poet himself. We are concerned now to note the effect of the spiritual experience.

The effect on Browning of his sudden awareness of Christ, of his intuitive contact with Christ, was that the truth slid into his soul and that his ordinary contacts were redeemed from criticism [1] and contempt.

[1] *Iago* . . . For I am nothing if not critical (*Othello*, Act II, Sc. I, 119).

He felt his fellowship with people he had despised, and joined in their worship.

The effect on Richard Rolle was to draw him so close to Christ that he feels towards Him as His own Mother might have felt and yet adores Him for the knightly course He has run.

The effect on Newman is to reveal the delicate care of an unending love that meets his own needs. He can rest in God.

III

THE SPIRITUAL IMPERATIVE

III

THE SPIRITUAL IMPERATIVE

I COME now to the mode of apprehension which
was next in my unusual experiences, the ' ghostly
understanding of clear and emphatic words,' [1] as
Lady Julian calls it. I may call the phenomenon the
Spiritual Imperative.

I

We will consider, first, the spiritual imperative
from the point of view of conduct.

St. Joan of Arc is the outstanding historical example
of the spiritual imperative. She saw visions, but
her historical importance lies 'in the fact· that she had
a ghostly understanding of clear and emphatic words
and carried out the command that was laid upon her.
She showed perseverance and was enabled to do what
she was told to do. She then desired to go home.

Historians—Anatole France [2] being the chief—
consider her visions and voices to have been due to
her abnormal physical condition. But even if she
were abnormal, one cannot discount all that
happened to her as of no practical importance. Ana-
tole France seems to hold that the directions given
to her were really the subjective illusions of an ab-

[1] *op. cit.*, p. 202.　　　　[2] See *Life of Joan of Arc, passim.*

normal person, and that what followed on her supposed revelations was due to the clever use made of her by others, who, not believing in her themselves, saw how the credulous enthusiasm of those who did believe in her would serve their own ends. Nevertheless, it was she and not they who initiated the campaign to relieve Orleans and to crown the King, and it was due to her vigour and pertinacity that the campaign was successful.

Bernard Shaw's opinion of her is clear in his Preface to *Saint Joan.* His opinion is that she was not abnormal physically or mentally. We may accept and admire her ' as a sane and shrewd country girl of extraordinary strength of mind and hardihood of body.' [1] But the visions and voices were illusory. Their wisdom was ' all Joan's own.' [2] This is shown by the occasions on which they failed her, notably during her trial, when they assured her that she would be ' rescued.' Her illusion persisted when she announced her ' relapse ' as dictated to her by her voices. But to Shaw ' all the popular religions in the world are made apprehensible by an array of legendary personages, with an Almighty Father, and sometimes a mother and divine child, as the central figures.' He allows that behind St. Catherine and the Holy Ghost ' there was a certain body of sound psychology,' as there is behind the ' quackeries,' which he describes under the heading of the ' Modern Education which Joan escaped.' [3]

Bernard Shaw goes back to an earlier psychologist for an epithet. He calls Joan a ' Galtonic visualizer.'

[1] *Saint Joan,* p. xxv. [2] *op. cit.,* p. xx. [3] *op. cit.,* pp. xviii and xix.

Seeing the play of *Saint Joan*, one might almost say that it was impossible for Bernard Shaw to write it—that the writer of the Preface could not have written the play; that his writing of the play is outside the range of ordinary psychological phenomena, and that he must have written the play when some Power outside himself had him in thrall, and that, therefore, the Power and not he is the real author. But Mr Shaw would be the first to laugh at so odd a theory. He was a visualizer when he wrote the play. There was no Power outside himself to ' dictate ' to him. He had only to sit down and he could make up *Saint Joan* out of his own head. He could see her perfectly. He could hear her speeches. And then he could dismiss these visualisations and these apparently authentic voices from his mind and say what he really thought about her in a Preface.

I have no more right to credit my own theory of the origin of his play, for he wrote the play, than I have to credit his theory of the origin of St. Joan's visions and voices, for she had the experiences. And being a sane and shrewd country girl, of extraordinary strength of mind, she was the kind of person to give a true account of them.

At any rate, her obedience to the spiritual imperative has wrought great things for us. Kipling says that the ' renaissance of strength and purpose at that hour (viz.: the ten years before the war) was due to Joan of Arc.[1] G. K. Chesterton, writing after 1914 about the effect of Joan of Arc upon the English, said [2]: ' We have done many foolish

[1] *Souvenirs of France*. pp. 24, 25.
[2] *A Short History of England* (1917), pp. 117 and 118.

things, but we have at least done one fine thing : we have whitewashed our worst enemies. If we have done this for a bold Scottish raider and a vigorous Virginian slave-holder, it may at least show that we are not likely to fail in our final appreciation of the one white figure in the motley processions of war. I believe there to be in modern England something like a universal enthusiasm on this subject. We have seen a great English critic write a book about this heroine, in opposition to a great French critic, solely in order to blame him for not having praised her enough. And I do not believe there lives an Englishman now, who, if he had the offer of being an Englishman then, would not discard his chance of riding as the crowned conqueror at the head of all the spears of Agincourt, if he could be that common soldier of whom tradition tells that he broke his spear asunder to bind it into a cross for Joan of Arc.'

As for the occasions on which Joan's voices ' failed ' her, I can gather out of my own insignificant experiences the cause of the failure. I attach importance to the fact that the spiritual imperative was involuntary. The command itself was amazing, when we consider who Joan was and that she was only eighteen years of age. But she obeyed it implicitly, in spite of many initial difficulties. When the issue had ratified her obedience, she wished to go home. The command came for a certain end, and when that end was reached, she knew that her task was over. I would recall to the sympathetic reader that at one point in my experience I was told, or seemed to be told, not to listen any more. I suggest that some such crisis came in Joan's experience when she begged to be allowed to go home. After that, her apprehending mind was not as it had been; it was unreliable. And the greatest trial of her character came *after* the unreliability of her apprehending mind. And, also, the greatest effect of what she did was not in the French victory but in her own defeat. She suffered, and out of her suffering has grown that ' something like a universal enthusiasm,' of which Chesterton speaks.

The spiritual imperative is the vital element of Quakerism. George Fox, being then twenty-two years of age, had in 1646 the ' central experience of his life,' as Elizabeth B. Emmott [1] calls it : ' When all my hopes in them, and in all men were gone, so that I had nothing outwardly to help me, nor could tell what to do; then, O ! then I heard a voice, which said, " *There is one, even Christ Jesus, that can speak to thy condition,*" and when I heard it my heart did leap for joy .... My desires after the Lord grew stronger, and zeal in the pure knowledge of God and of Christ alone, without the help of any man, book or writing. For though I read the Scriptures that spake of Christ and of God, yet I knew Him not but by revelation, as He who hath the key did open, and as the Father of Life drew me to His Son by His Spirit ....' [2]

He was ' commanded ' to turn people to that inward light, spirit and grace.[3] He felt that Christ could speak not only to his condition—of helplessness

---

[1] *A Short History of Quakerism* (1922), p. 83.
[2] *Journal*, 1st Ed., p. 8.   [3] *Ibid.*, p. 23.

and of not knowing what to do—but to the condition of others. The avoidance of soldiership and the determination not to bear arms followed. George Fox lived through a time of civil war. The time also seemed to him to be patient of unreality in external religion and of insincere customs and ceremonies in social life. ' Moreover, when the Lord sent me forth into the world, He forbade me to put off my hat to any, high or low. And I was required to Thee and Thou all men and women, without any respect to rich or poor, great or small. And as I travelled up and down, I was not to bid people good-morrow or good-evening; neither might I bow or scrape with my leg to anyone; and this made the sects or professions to rage.'

These ' requirements ' have tended to obscure the vital element. They also give the impression that George Fox was touchy and critical, which William Penn says expressly that he was not. Neither was he a busybody nor a self-seeker, but ' so meek, contented, modest, easy, steady, tender, that it was a pleasure to be in his company.'

The determination not to bear arms, though a negative principle, is one of immense positive importance. The War of 1914—1918 was a sign of the failure of modern civilisation to work out the law of love in industrial and national relationships. I am not now concerned with the questions of self-defence and disarmament. But it is obvious that if this negative principle of Quakerism obtained universal recognition we should be rid of one great bogey of fear.

Isaac Penington, born in 1616, the son of one of Charles I's judges, is called by W. C. Braithwaite [1] ' the Quaker mystic.' He married the widow of Sir William Springett in 1654 and both he and his wife found in ' the Quaker experience of an indwelling Christ ' that for which their souls had been thirsting. Penington's writings afford the best clue that the Quakerism of the seventeeth century had to give of its religious faith. Penington is the author of a saying, to which I must refer in a later chapter : ' Every truth is a shadow except the last. But every truth is substance in its own place, though it be but a shadow in another place. And the shadow is a true shadow, as the substance is a true substance.' [2] This saying emphasises the human response to the spiritual imperative, a response involving preparation, seeking, which closes in the ' experience ' for which the soul thirsts.

These early Quakers gave bold expression to the spiritual imperative ; they spoke as clearly as Joan of Arc.

But others, who keep silence about God and the soul, may nevertheless have a ghostly understanding of clear and emphatic words. This seems to have been the case with Marshal Foch, a man of irrefragable religious conviction, to whom what the Quakers called ' external religion ' was a matter of great moment, for he went to Mass on every morning that it was possible. An observer [3] has written of him : ' I noticed that when first one addressed Marshal

---

[1] *The Second Period of Quakerism*, p. 397.
[2] Quoted by Dean Inge in *Introduction to ' Lyra Mystica,'* p. xxvi.
[3] *The Times*, July 7th, 1928.

Foch he seemed most inclined to listen. His manner was courteous and quiet, his look grave; his mind seemed patient, receptive, unresponsive—but this at least was misleading, for in fact every question received an answer. Sometimes an interval elapsed; sometimes the retort was instantaneous. *Instinct seemed to be at work as much as intellect,*[1] and when he spoke one occasionally had the feeling that a power outside and greater than himself was speaking through him.'[2]

I have sometimes wondered if one could dare to think of the faultless apprehension of Christ Jesus in terms of a Voice. He is reported[3] as saying : ' And the word which ye hear is not mine but my Father's which sent me ' (καὶ ὁ λόγος ὃν ἀκούετε οὐκ ἔστιν ἐμὸς ἀλλὰ τοῦ πέμψαντός με Πατρός). It is remarkable to find ἀκούετε, as if He ignored Himself altogether. When He was near the end of His hard dying He may have listened for the Voice and not heard it. That would account for the desolating sense of dereliction to which He gave utterance.

II

§ i

William Blake is the outstanding example of the Spiritual Imperative in English Literature. His

[1] Italics mine.

[2] The observer uses ' instinct ' in the same sense as it was used of Lord Roberts (see p. 123), or as in *Christmas Eve* (xvi) of Shakespeare, ' whose insight makes all others dim,' and is yet comparable to the ' gift ' of a bat discerning ' some pitch-dark cavern's fifty turns.' Foch seems to have ' waited for ' some of his own answers, which persuades me of something more definite than ' instinct ' implies.

[3] St. John xiv, 24.

name for it is ' Dictation.' He reserves this name for
his ' Giant Forms ' poems, but he is the most consist-
ent of all believers in Intuition, whether for Poetry or
Painting; and ' Dictation ' is only a form of Intuition.
He distinguishes between ' Objects of Reasoning '
and ' Objects of Intuition.' Demonstration, Simili-
tude and Harmony are objects of Reasoning.
Invention, Identity and Melody are objects of
Intuition.[1]

Obedience to the Spiritual Imperative is the key to
Blake. We will consider it, first, in regard to his ' new
scriptures.'

He writes (April 25, 1803) to his friend and em-
ployer, Thomas Butts, from his cottage in Felpham :
' But none can know the Spiritual Acts of my three
years' Slumber on the banks of the Ocean, unless he
has seen them in the Spirit, or unless he should read
My long Poem descriptive of those Acts; for I have
in these three years composed an immense number of
verses on One Grand Theme, Similar to Homer's Iliad
or Milton's Paradise Lost, the Persons and Machinery
intirely new to the Inhabitants of Earth (some of the
Persons Excepted). I have written this Poem from
immediate Dictation, twelve or sometimes twenty or
thirty lines at a time, without Premeditation & even
against my Will; the Time it has taken in writing
was thus render'd Non Existent, and an immense
Poem Exists which seems to be the Labour of a long
Life, all produc'd without Labour or Study. I men-

---

[1] All the quotations of Blake's writings are taken from *The Poetry and
Prose of William Blake*, ed. by Geoffrey Keynes, complete in one volume
(Nonesuch Press, 1927). They will be referred to as ' Nonesuch ' and the
pages indicated. This from *Marginalia on Reynolds's Discourses* is
Nonesuch, 1008.

tion this to shew you what I think the Grand Reason of my being brought down here.'

The poem is a descriptive poem of his spiritual acts, which he assumes might be known to others without reading the poem. They might know ' in the spirit,' because *Milton,* the poem to which he refers, is a true interpretation of spiritual processes. Creation demands fulfilment. Creation issues in joy. Man fulfils himself in obedience to his own nature and endowments. The system of life must be in a constant advance, until man is united or identified with God—loses and finds himself in God. He can only do so by a recognition of the reality of his own sinfulness and the truth of his own contacts. Then he knows that ' the Spirit of Jesus is continual forgiveness of Sin,' [1] and that his own contacts demand mutual forgiveness.

Blake had heard the Christian religion preached as a series of negatives. The ' moral virtues ' were prohibitions. The law was not forgiveness but penalty. But he understands Vice as a negative. ' It does not signify what the laws of Kings and Priests have called Vice; we who are philosophers ought not to call the Staminal Virtues by the same name that we call the omissions of intellect springing from poverty.' [2]

This guides us to the apprehending mind and its richness through the training of experience. Intuitions are authentic to the experienced ear of the good and faithful servant. The poor and ill-nourished mind that cannot catch God's whispers omits action

[1] Nonesuch, 550.   [2] Nonesuch, 932.

and hinders others. So also each thing is its own cause and its own effect. It is the effect that matters, but if we understand truly the effect we are acquainted with its cause. If the effect is positive we can trace it back to the Holy Word; it is the Holy Word in action. If the effect is to hinder (' Murder is Hindering Another. Theft is hindering Another ')—and he who hinders another omits his own duty at the same time—then the cause is poverty, not of the Holy Word but of the understanding, and vice is an omission of the intellect springing from poverty.[1]

The origin of the mistake of Lavater and his contemporaries about Sin and the Moral Virtues lies in the supposition that ' Woman's Love is Sin; in consequence all the Loves and Graces with them are Sins.'

This, gathered out of his writings, may perhaps be taken as a brief account of Blake's ' spiritual acts ' during his three years' slumber on the banks of the Ocean. The poem descriptive of these spiritual acts was ' dictated ' to him.

He is even more explicit in his address to the public concerning his next poem, *Jerusalem, the Emanation of the Giant Albion*. He first expresses his hope that the reader will be with him, ' wholly one in Jesus our Lord, who is the God of Fire and Lord of Love, to whom the Ancients look'd and saw his day afar off, with trembling and amazement.'[2] The poem is headed : ' Μονος ὁ Ιεσους.' There is a partially erased passage : ' I fear the best . . . in Jesus whom we . . . ,' which seems to indicate that Jesus dictated to him.

---

[1] *cf. Plotinus*, Ennead VI, 7, 2.   [2] Nonesuch, 550.

' We who dwell on Earth can do nothing of our-selves; everything is conducted by Spirits, no less than Digestion or Sleep . . . When this Verse was first dictated to me, I consider'd a Monotonous Cadence, like that used by Milton & Shakespeare & all writers of English Blank Verse, derived from the modern bondage of Rhyming, to be a necessary and indispensible part of Verse. But I soon found that in the mouth of a true Orator such monotony was not only awkward, but as much a bondage as rhyme itself. I therefore have produced a variety in every line, both of cadences and number of syllables. Every word and every letter is studied and put into its place . . .'

It is difficult to determine the activities that went with ' dictation.' The Verse was ' dictated ' to him, and he was, at first, inclined to reject it in favour of Blank Verse. But he found the new Verse suitable to a ' true Orator,' as if he heard the lines spoken.

His hint about digestion and sleep may afford some clue to the process of writing. Both these other pro-cesses demand some correspondence in man himself and involve a determination not to interfere with what the ' Spirits conduct.'

I am not concerned primarily with the doctrine of these new scriptures of Blake. D. Saurat and J. Middleton Murry have made close studies of it.[1] Murry asserts that ' the system of orthodox Christian-ity was incapable of containing, without distortion, the vast and simple synthesis which was Blake's message.' But Blake in glimpses is more revealing than Blake in symbols.

[1] *Blake and Modern Thought* by Denis Saurat (1929) and *William Blake* by J. Middleton Murry (1933).

Arise, you little glancing wings, and sing your infant joy!
Arise, and drink your bliss, for everything that lives is
    holy! [1]

Thou perceivest the Flowers put forth their precious
    Odours,
And none can tell how from so small a center comes such
    sweets,
Forgetting that within that Center Eternity expands
Its ever during doors . . . [2]

O Lord & Saviour, have the Gods of the Heathen pierced
    thee,
Or hast thou been pierced in the House of thy Friends?
Art thou alive, & livest thou for evermore? or art thou
Not [Nought] but a delusive shadow, a thought that liveth
    not?
Babel mocks, saying there is no God nor Son of God,
That thou, O Human Imagination, O Divine Body, art all
A delusion; but I know thee, O Lord, when thou arisest
    upon
My weary eyes, even in this dungeon & this iron mill. [3]

        . . . every kindness to another is a little Death
In the Divine Image . . . [4]

I do not know what Murry means by ' the system
of orthodox Christianity.' The vital heart of Blake's
religion is a deep and aweful devotion to Jesus Christ,
and none has indicated with a greater magic of words
the truth of Him. I need not speak now of Blake's
joy in created things, akin to that of his ' Lord &
Saviour,' or his enthusiasm for children, but it should
be noticed how closely he follows the New Testament
writers in his interpretation of Christ's Death, in his
view of the Sacrament of Holy Communion, and in
his expression of the transcendence and familiarity of
Jesus.

    Christ's great kindness was in His Death, and it

---

[1] Nonesuch, p. 215.   [2] Nonesuch, p. 526.
[3] Nonesuch, p. 665.   [4] Nonesuch, p. 746.

was a Death in the Divine Image, and every kindness
to another is therefore a ' little ' Death in the Divine
Image.

Professor Housman in his Leslie Stephen lecture on
The Name and Nature of Poetry (1933) quotes from
Blake with omissions. He takes a fragmentary poem,
beginning,

> My Spectre around me day and night . . .

and stops after eight stanzas. He says that the verses
' probably possessed for Blake a meaning, and his
students think they have found it; but the meaning is
a poor foolish disappointing thing in comparison
with the verses themselves.' Housman stops short
of this stanza:

> & Throughout all Eternity
> I forgive you, you forgive me.
> As our dear Redeemer said:
> ' This the Wine & this the Bread ' [1]

This is the crowning stanza. Is Blake's divine
intuition linking *mutual* forgiveness with the Sacra-
ment of Christ's Body and Blood ' a poor disappoint-
ing thing?'

Again: ' Lastly take this stanza, addressed " to
the Accuser who is the God of this World."

> Tho' thou art worship'd by the names divine
> Of Jesus and Jehovah, thou art still
> The Son of Morn in weary Night's decline,—
> The lost traveller's dream under the hill.

It purports to be theology: what theological sense,
if any, it may have, I cannot imagine and feel no wish
to learn: it is pure and self-existent poetry, which
leaves no room in me for anything besides.'

[1] Nonesuch, pp. 105, 106.

I agree that this stanza is not far from being the best ever written, but the effect of it as pure poetry arises from Blake's love for Jesus, and his feeling that the more familiar Jesus is and the more He means to men in the deepest places of their beings the more transcendent He is.

The stanza is quoted from [Epilogue] *The Gates of Paradise*.[1] This is the whole of the Epilogue:

> To The Accuser who is
> The God of This World
> Truly, My Satan, thou art but a Dunce,
> And dost not know the Garment from the Man.
> Every Harlot was a Virgin once,
> Nor can'st thou ever change Kate into Nan.
>
> Tho' thou art Worship'd by the Names Divine
> Of Jesus & Jehovah, thou art still
> The Son of Morn in weary Night's decline,
> The lost Traveller's Dream under the Hill.

Blake mocks at Satan for a dunce because he failed to recognize the essential goodness of creation. He thought he could foil God. He also reckoned without the Redeemer, the God who is not of this world, but who visits and redeems His people. The meaning or theology of the first stanza may be found in Genesis I or the Prologue to St. John's Gospel, and of the second stanza in the very familiar words of another great poetic utterance: ' through the tender mercy of our God, whereby the Dayspring from on high hath visited us, to give light to them that sit in darkness and in the shadow of death and to guide our feet into the way of peace.'

Blake's hope is in Jesus. If there is any apparent contradiction it is reconciled through Jesus.[2] He con-

---

[1] Nonesuch, p. 763.   [2] *Milton*, p. 486.

verses with Jesus; ' his words are dictated by Jesus; he is one with God (' as man with man ') and yet he looks to Jesus as the Friend of Sinners, He being ' all virtue,' and through Him and in Him finds continual forgiveness. He is so familiar with Jesus that he knows what He looks like.[1] The laughing Jesus is the child's Jesus. The ' Jesus ' Blake hates is the ' creeping Jesus.' [2] Jesus is God revealed in the intelligible terms of our humanity.[3]

§ ii

Blake's revolt against the ' moral virtues ' is really a belief in instinct, impulse, intuition, the Human Imagination which is the Divine Body of Jesus, Jesus the intuitive Person (' He acted from impulse not from rules '), God the Light, or, in other words, the Spiritual Imperative. He is fighting against repressions and the view of marriage which denies joy and suggests that desire is evil in itself. ' They suppose that Woman's Love is Sin; in consequence all the Loves & Graces with them are Sins.'[4]

And still more plainly :

> ABSTINENCE sows sand all over
> The ruddy limbs & flaming hair,
> But Desire Gratified
> Plants fruits of life & beauty there [5]

Again :

> LOVE to faults is always blind,
> Always is to joy inclin'd,
> Lawless, wing'd, & unconfin'd,
> And breaks all chains from every mind.

[1] Nonesuch, p. 893. See also *Marginalia on Lavater's Aphorisms*. Nos. 16, 383. Nonesuch, pp. 903, 916.
[2] Nonesuch, p. 135. [3] p. 120. [4] See p. 87. [5] Nonesuch, p. 99

Deceit to secresy confin'd,
Lawful, cautious and refin'd;
To everything but interest blind,
And forges fetters for the mind.[1]

When he went to the Garden of Love he found a Chapel built in the midst with ' Thou shalt not ' over the door, and for the rest of the Garden—

I saw it was filled with graves,
And tomb-stones where flowers should be;
And Priests in black gowns were walking their rounds,
And binding with briers my joys and desires [2]

The most moving of all his poems on this theme is *A Little Girl Lost* [3] with this stanza prefixed :

Children of the future Age
Reading this indignant page,
Know that in a former time
Love! sweet Love! was thought a crime.

John Galsworthy has taken up the theme in *Saint's Progress,* and, though his treatment lacks the burning indignation of Blake and is cautious and refined, realising the spiritual dilemma of the Priest in black gown walking his round, he shows that the ' children of the future age ' are reading life as Blake read it.[4]

Blake's ' rebel ' poem, *The Everlasting Gospel,* expresses his abhorrence of principles (here called the Moral Virtues) and his belief in individual inspiration. The poem is fragmentary. What can be collected together from the sections of the Rossetti MS. and two additional small sheets of paper shows that Blake started again on the section beginning ' Was Jesus Humble ? ' He seems also to have been dissatisfied

[1] Nonesuch, p. 96.   [2] Nonesuch, p. 74.
[3] *Songs of Experience,* Nonesuch, p. 78.
[4] Blake had his lapses into lewdness (Nonesuch, p. 88) and there were times when he considered woman's love as a temptation (p. 106).

with the section marked *e* in the Nonesuch Edition, beginning ' Was Jesus Chaste? ' He repeats parts of section *d* in section *i*, but this may be because he had forgotten what he had written. All spontaneous writers forget. They forget their own words more easily than they forget the words of other men, because their own words are not their own. In this poem Blake repeats the startling conviction in *Auguries of Innocence*,

> If the Sun & Moon should doubt,
> They'd immediately go out,

in the form,

> Humility is only doubt,
> And does the Sun & Moon blot out,

showing that the interpretation of the first passage is individual, and that the ' going out ' is of the mind —' Mind is the first and most direct thing in our experience; all else is remote inference.' [1]

In his little prose-preface to *The Everlasting Gospel*, Blake insists again on the true Gospel: ' There is not one Moral Virtue that Jesus Inculcated but Plato & Cicero did Inculcate before Him; what then did Christ Inculcate? Forgiveness of Sins. This alone is the Gospel, & this is the Life & Immortality brought to light by Jesus, Even the Covenant of Jehovah, which is This: If you forgive one another your Trespasses, so shall Jehovah forgive you, That he himself may dwell among you; but if you Avenge, you Murder the Divine Image, & he cannot dwell among you; because you Murder him he arises again, & you deny that he is Arisen, & are blind to Spirit.'

[1] *Science and the Unseen World* by A. S. Eddington, p. 37.

He had joined the ' forgiveness of sins ' with the Sacrament or the Sacrifice of ' our dear Redeemer.' This is the same thing looked at from the other side : the Sacrifice was a Murder, followed by a rising again, and the denial of the rising is blindness to Spirit. This that took place in time—

> He took on Sin in the Virgin's womb
> And put it off on the Cross & Tomb—

is somehow part of the Eternal and is going on now.

But the remainder of the poem is designed, if there is any design, to show that the Vision of Christ ' that thou dost see ' is not Blake's vision, but his vision's greatest enemy. And as the Moral Virtues all begin in the Accusations of Sin, he attacks the Moral Virtues in turn. That Jesus should merely display the Moral Virtues and not the originality of God's Son offends everything in him to which he attaches spiritual importance. For example, he pours scorn on the conventional idea of humility, which is more like the 'umbleness of Uriah Heep than a quality of Jesus, and speaks thus of the Crucifixion :

> But, when Jesus was Crucified,
> Then was perfected his glitt'ring pride :
> In three Nights he devour'd his prey.
> And still he devours the Body of Clay;
> For dust & Clay is the Serpent's meat,
> Which never was made for Man to Eat.

His work of devouring the Body of Clay still goes on.

The poem ' was never finished, nor did Blake give any indication of how he intended it to be arranged.' [1]

Judging from my own small performances and the

---

[1] Nonesuch, p. 130.

fact that *after* writing his Didactic and Symbolical Works, Blake began a poem with the title, *The Everlasting Gospel* (1818), I entertain a theory that he became dissatisfied with his new scriptures and attempted to set forth his ' beliefs ' and his view of Jesus and the way of redemption in clear and intelligible language. Perhaps, in the end, he realised the futility of re-interpreting the Gospel, except in those ' songs ' which had been given him to write. A poet is not a ' teacher.' Didacticism is not his province. Even in Jesus the power and love that move us to praying do not spring from what He taught of moral virtue or religious duty but from what He was and is in Himself, shown in His kindness and friendliness and in that Death in the Divine Image which was His great good deed for the world. We can feel the urge and thrill of Jesus in Blake's songs, and more in ' Tyger! Tyger! ' than in *The Everlasting Gospel*.

§ iii

Just before Blake fell back dead in the very middle of singing a song,[1] he said, to his wife, of his own songs, ' My beloved, they are not mine—no—they are not mine.'

But sometimes—indeed over a period of twenty years—he was plagued by a spectrous fiend,[2] who was the ruin of his labours. ' O the distress I have undergone, and my poor wife with me: incessantly labouring and incessantly spoiling what I had done

[1] It should not be forgotten that Blake sang his songs to his own spontaneous notes, and, also, that he considered the plates an integral part of his work.

[2] Nonesuch, p. 409.

well.' He reduced this fiend to his station. ' He is become my servant who domineered over me, he is even as a brother who was mine enemy.'

I think, from his use of the word ' spectre ' in other places, that this enemy who could become as a servant or a brother was the embodiment of intellect or reason divorced from intuition. But the fiend may be the spirit of doubt or personal ambition or the domineering false spirit of self-estimation with the consequent resentment of the reputation of others. The poet who knows he is greater than he is reputed to be, or a painter who feels that his art has a right quality as distinct from the false quality of the ' virtuous ass,' is liable to be plagued by such a fiend.

When Blake was free, he wrote poems that have the hush of listening angels just before God speaks. He seems to have felt the wonder himself. In the middle of a satirical new kind of novel called *An Island in the Moon* [1] he puts into the mouth of Mr Obtuse Angle this song :

Upon a holy thursday, their innocent faces clean,
The children walking two & two in grey and blue & green,
Grey-headed beadles walk'd before with wands as white as snow,
Till into the high dome of Paul's they like thames' waters flow.

O what a multitude they seem'd, these flowers of London town !
Seated in companies, they sit with radiance all their own.
The hum of multitudes were there, but multitudes of lambs,
Thousands of little girls & boys raising their innocent hands.

[1] Written about 1787. The song is reproduced in *The Songs of Innocence* with the alteration of a word or two. Nonesuch, p. 884.

> Then like a mighty wind they raise to heav'n thc voice
> of song,
> Or like harmonious thunderings the seats of heav'n
> among.
> Beneath them sit the rev'rend men, the guardians of the
> poor;
> Then cherish pity lest you drive an angel from the door.

' After this,' he goes on, ' *they all sat silent for a quarter of an hour*,[1] & Mrs. Nannicantipot said, " It puts me in Mind of my mother's song." '

This ' mother's song ' is *The Nurse's Song* as found in the *Songs of Innocence* and Quid follows with *The Little Boy Lost*.

' Here nobody could sing any longer, till Tilly Lally pluck'd up a spirit & he sung :

> " I say, you Joe,
> Throw us the ball.
> I've a good mind to go
> And leave you all . . ." '

The wonder of Blake is sometimes seen in a single spontaneous word or phrase :

> Hungry clouds *swag* on the deep [2]
>
> Nor shall my Sword *sleep* in my hand [3]
>
> And a little lovely *Moony Night* [4]
>
> Iron tears and groans of lead
> Bind around my aking head.[5]
>
> One standing in the Porches of the Sun [6]
>
> Or who will exchange his new born child
> For the dog at the wintry door [7]
>
> For a tear is an Intellectual thing [8]

---

[1] Italics mine.
[2] The Marriage of Heaven and Hell, p. 190.
[3] Milton, p. 465.
[4] The Crystal Cabinet, p. 116.
[5] *Ibid.*, p. 107.
[6] To Mrs Anna Flaxman, p. 104.
[7] *Ibid.*, p. 103.
[8] The Grey Monk, p. 118

Sometimes in a stanza:

> The sword sung on the barren heath,
> The sickle in the fruitful field:
> The sword he sung a song of death,
> But could not make the sickle yield.[1]

We may perhaps be able to see what Dictation involved by examining the two drafts of *The Tyger*.

The first draft contains seven stanzas; the poem in *Songs of Experience*, six. I conceive that as Blake was writing down the poem he came to a stop at

> What dread hand and what dread feet . . .

These words sounded back to him as if they were a question:

> And when thy heart began to beat
> What dread hand and what dread feet . . . ?

He paused for a long time. What could that feeling of a question imply? Then he went on—another stanza:

> Could fetch it from the furnace deep
> And in thy horrid ribs dare steep
> In the well of sanguine woe?
> In what clay and in what mould
> Were thy eyes of fury roll'd?

Very uneasy! Well, go on.

> Where the hammer? Where the chain?
> In what furnace was thy brain?
> What the anvil? What dread grasp
> Dare its deadly terrors clasp?

Then came something that startled him:

> When the stars threw down their spears
> And water'd heaven with their tears . . .

These verses came quickly and firmly.

[1] The Grey Monk, p. 99.

D . . . He could not be sure of the first word that was to follow. Finally he wrote:

> Dare he . . . (What?)
> Dare he laugh his work to see?
> Dare he who made the lamb make thee?
>
> Tyger, Tyger, burning bright
> In the forests of the night,
> What immortal hand & eye
> Dare frame thy fearful symmetry?

He read through what he had written. He had hesitated several times. He had doubted. He knew that if he doubted he was lost.

Then—after what interval one cannot tell—he took a sheet of paper and determined to begin again without looking at the old copy.[1]

> Tyger! (That exclamation mark made a difference)
> Tyger! Tyger! burning bright
> In the forest of the night,
> What immortal hand or eye
> Could (Yes, of course) frame thy fearful symmetry?
>
> In what distant deeps or skies
> Burnt the fire of thine eyes?
> On what wings dare he aspire?
> What the hand dare seize the fire?
>
> And what shoulder and what art
> Could twist the sinews of thy heart?[2]
> And when thy heart began to beat,
> What dread hand . . .

Here, once more, was the same insistent feeling of a question. He yielded to it:

> What dread hand? & what dread feet?
> When the stars threw down their spears,
> And water'd heaven with their tears

[1] This *must* have been so, because we have the two versions.

[2] This has reference to the potter (thrower) at work. As the clay is spinning round and the thrower is fashioning it, great strength and effort of the shoulder are demanded, especially if the vessel is a large one. *Cf.* Ecclesiasticus 38, 30:

> He will fashion the clay with his arm,
> And will bend its strength in front of his feet.

D . . . (Yes)
Did he smile his work to see?
Did he who made the Lamb make thee?

Tyger! Tyger! burning bright
In the forest of the night,
What immortal hand or eye
Dare (Yes, 'Dare,' this time) frame thy fearful
    symmetry?

This obedience to the Spiritual Imperative—to God speaking ' within the unfathom'd caverns of my Ear ' [1]—was at least as great an abandonment in faith as the act of a man who accepts his dictations for conduct. We may also begin to perceive that, for Blake at least, the whole poetic experience, whether in the glowing confusion or in the act of writing, was akin to the experience of those Angels of His who hearken to the voice of God's word.

III

I will refer briefly to the poetry of Gerard Manley Hopkins.[2] He died in the same year as Browning (1889), but the book of his poems, edited by his friend, Robert Bridges, was not issued until 1918. A second edition was published in 1930, with an appendix of additional poems and a critical introduction by Charles Williams.

§ i

In an unfinished poem called *The Woodlark* [3] Gerard Hopkins gives an account of his poetic habit, in which he emphasizes the necessity of obedience to

[1] Nonesuch, p. 551.

[2] I wish to acknowledge the help, for this section, of Miss E. Holmes, a poet as well as a student of poetry.

[3] Second Edition, p. 83.

the Spiritual Imperative. He identifies himself with
the lark : ' The Skylark is my cousin.' There is a
cry within directing him :

>   . . . when the cry within
> Says Go on then I go on
> Till the longing is less and the good gone.

He brings in a new element : the effect of saying. The
force of Go on is not to be denied. He must attempt
to set down his poetic experience. He goes on till
the longing is less and the good gone. The passion
to write is less urgent, and the writing down of what
was stirring within him has somehow been the death
of it—not for others but for himself. But he must not
repine at that ; he must obey the voice :

> But down drop, if it says Stop,
> To the all-a-leaf of the treetop
> And after that off the bough.

This is the same kind of cry as Blake heard when
he was writing *Milton* : ' Go on,' and then, after
twelve or twenty or thirty lines, ' Stop.' Why Go
on or Stop unless to mark the beginning or the end
of the inspiration—of the thing breathed in ? The
cry is heard within ; the scope is decided from without.
The skylark did not make himself ; he came into
being.

He mentions the ' scope ' in another fragment, ' On
a piece of music.' [1] The artist's scope is given to
him :

> He swept what scope he was
> To sweep and must obey

It is only within his being's bent that he is able to

[1] Second Edition, p. 85.

change in choice. As a poet or musician there is
neither right nor wrong for him,[1]

> No more than red and blue.
> No more than Re and Mi,
> Or sweet the golden glue
> That's built for by the bee.

The bee builds for the golden glue; the golden glue
itself is not the bee's doing : it ' comes.'

The man, however, is concerned with right and
wrong. And for this,

> What makes the man and what
> The man within that makes:
> Ask whom he serves or not serves
> And what side he takes.

The original impulse of the poet is to most careful
obedience to the Spiritual Imperative, but we must
take into account the quality of the receiving mind and
its *askesis* for poetry. The *askesis* for poetry is
different from the *askesis* for the man. Gerard Hop-
kins had a notable *askesis* for poetry,[2] but he was a
priest of the Society of Jesus and considered the
askesis for the man of supreme importance. Shelley
also had a notable *askesis* for poetry to subserve his
impassioned intuition, but his *askesis* for the man was
nothing.

Gerard Hopkins determined when he became a
Jesuit in 1868 not to write poetry except by the wish
of his superiors. He wrote a few presentation pieces,
of which *Rosa Mystica* is certainly one, and then
happened in the Winter of 1875 the wreck of the

---

[1] *cf. Esprit de Vinet* (Astier) ii, p. 400, quoted by Henri Bremond,
op. cit. p. 214.

[2] *Poems of Gerard Manley Hopkins,* 2nd Ed. Author's Preface.

Deutschland. She was wrecked in the mouth of the Thames and five Franciscan nuns aboard of her were drowned. Hopkins wrote to a friend (Oct. 5, 1878): ' I was affected by the account and happening to say so to my rector he said he wished someone would write a poem on the subject. On this hint I set to work, and though my hand was out at first, produced one. I had long had haunting my ear the echo of a new rhythm which now I realised on paper . . . .'

Robert Bridges speaks, as Ben Jonson might have spoken, of ' the labour spent on this great metrical experiment,' but when we begin the poem we do not think of a metrical experiment or how the poet harnesses his strong words or if he is writing in Running Rhythm or Sprung Rhythm ; we are carried away by the rush and glory of his release into poetry :

> Thou mastering me
> God ! giver of breath and bread;
> World's strand, sway of the sea;
> Lord of living and dead;
> Thou hast bound bones and veins in me, fastened me flesh,
> And after it almost unmade, what with dread,
> Thy doing; and dost thou touch me afresh?
> Over again I feel thy finger and find thee.

And, thereafter, for nine stanzas more, he speaks of Christ and himself, and we have only to simplify (if it were possible) his panting hard-driven battering bright language to feel ourselves again with Jesus and Blake. Speaking of his Master : Not out of his bliss springs the stress felt,

> It dates from day
> Of his going in Galilee;
> Warm-laid grave of a womb-life grey;
> Manger, maiden's knee;

The dense and driven Passion, and frightful sweat;
Hence the discharge of it, there its swelling to be,
    Though felt before, though in high flood yet—
What none would have known of it, only the heart, being
    hard at bay,
        Is out with it!

§ ii

I have spoken of a new element acknowledged in Hopkins's poetic habit—the dispersion or death of the poetic experience through writing it down : ' Till the longing is less and the *good gone.*'

But Hopkins, though he felt the poetic urge as strongly as any poet, had a better habit than the habit of poetry. It was the habit of silence, of praying at its highest, when the intuition is of God as present; and it was for this intuition that he was qualifying himself. The poetic experience is dispersed in *saying;* but this experience is incommunicable and serves for the fulness of life.

His poem, *The Habit of Perfection,*[1] is not a series of paradoxes. The ' Elected Silence ' does sing to him, but it is a song that cannot be uttered. Wordsworth speaks of our being ' laid asleep in body.' [2] Hopkins speaks better. The senses, or what correspond to the senses, (there is σῶμα ψυχικόν even as there is σῶμα πνευματικόν), are put to proper uses : the ears for hearing, the lips for eloquence, the eyes for light, the palate for food, the nostrils for their ' relish,' the feet for walking and the hands for handling; and all within this ' stillness of the spirit.' He is a man who has surrendered himself.

[1] *op. cit.,* p. 8.   [2] *Tintern Abbey.*

> Shape nothing lips; be lovely dumb:
> It is the shut, the curfew sent
> From there where all surrenders come
> Which only makes you eloquent.

Yet along this path lies sometimes—St. John of the Cross would say, always—a dark place.

In a letter to Robert Bridges of September 1, 1885, Hopkins wrote : ' I shall shortly have some sonnets to send you, five or more. Four of these came like inspirations unbidden and against my will.[1] And in the life I lead now, which is one of a continually jaded and harassed mind, if in any leisure I try to do something I make no way—nor with my work, alas ! but so it must be.'

Perhaps the deepest darkness is indicated in the following [2] :

> I am gall, I am heartburn. God's most deep decree
> Bitter would have me taste; my taste was me;
> Bones built in me, flesh filled, blood brimmed the curse.
>   Selfyeast of spirit a dull dough sours. I see
> The lost are like this, and their scourge to be
> As I am mine, their sweating selves; but worse.

The ' good ' goes when the poet speaks, is somehow lost. But may not the poet speak to the man's relief? If by ' saying ' he disperses for himself the ' good ' of the poetic experience, may he not also by saying help to rid himself of this terrible darkness of the spirit? Having been brought into this temptation, he is also shown the way out and driven to take it against his will. If any reader objects to the word ' bring ' I can only appeal to the Lord's Prayer and to the poet's own words, written in his diary : ' But

---

[1] cf. Blake, p. 85.   [2] op. cit., p. 65.

in all this our Lord goes His own way.' [1]   The Divine
Imperative is final.

IV

In the light thrown by these two poets upon their
poetic habit we may be able to interpret the habit of
Plotinus.[2]   Porphyry of Tyre, writing on his life and
the arrangement of his work, says : ' Plotinus could
not bear to go back on his work even for one re-
reading ; and, indeed, the condition of his sight would
scarcely allow it : his handwriting was slovenly ; he
misjoined his words ; he cared nothing about spelling ;
his one concern was for the idea : in these habits, to
our general surprise, he remained unchanged to the
very end.

' He used to work out his design mentally from
first to last : when he came to set down his ideas, he
wrote at one jet all that he had stored in mind as
though he were copying from a book.

' Interrupted, perhaps, by someone entering on
business, he never lost hold of his plan ; he was able
to meet all the demands of the conversation and still
keep his own train of thought clearly before him ;
when he was free again, he never looked over what he
had previously written—his sight, it has been men-
tioned, did not allow of such re-reading—but he

[1] *Gerard Manley Hopkins* by G. F. Lahey, p. 138.
[2] Plotinus was born in Egypt, A.D. 205, at Lycopolis, and died near
Rome, A.D. 270. See Porphyry : On the Life of Plotinus and the
Arrangement of his Work (Stephen MacKenna's Translation, 1917).
Plotinus's book is *The Enneads*. Mr MacKenna died on March 8, 1934.
I feel as if I had lost a friend. His translation of *The Enneads* has
given me many happy hours.

linked on what was to follow as if no distraction had occurred.'

I think we may leave out consideration of his sight, because ' he could not bear to go back over his work.' I suggest that he did not work out his design mentally from first to last. The ideas or ' spiritual acts ' (as Blake called them) were somehow in his mind, but for indication of them I suggest that when he came to write he surrendered himself to a ' Being of more divine degree,' and without hesitation wrote down words that he recognized for the expression (or, indication) of an idea *after* he had written them or in the very act of writing them. That would account for the ease and readiness with which he turned to someone who interrupted him and for the ease and readiness with which he resumed his writing. He felt he had no need to keep his own train of thought because he was actually writing without the immediate process of thinking. The person entering on business interrupted him only in a time-sense. Plotinus went back to his book and continued as before. There was no need to look over what he had previously written, because he was writing at ' dictation.'

Porphyry does hint at such an explanation. He says [1] : ' Thus Plotinus had for indwelling spirit a

---

[1] cf. *Confessions of St Augustine*, iii, 11 : ' Thou wert more inward to me than my most inward part and higher than the highest.'

It is worth noticing that Plotinus in his saying about the Beings who were in the habit of coming to him has expressed the complementary (and *essentially* Christian) attitude to that expressed by St Augustine (Conf : vii, 23) : ' and thus with the flash of one trembling glance it arrived at That Which Is.' If the above be a true interpretation of Plotinus' utterance, we see him nearer the Christian Agape than the Greek Eros : That Which Is comes upon the soul.

Being of the more divine degree, and he kept his own divine spirit unceasingly intent upon that inner presence. It was this preoccupation that led him to write his treatise upon *Our Tutelary Spirit,* an essay in the explanation of the differences among spirit-guides.'

Porphyry goes on, still with the same essential bewilderment : ' Amelius was scrupulous in observing the day of the New Moon and other holy days, and once asked Plotinus to join in some such celebration. Plotinus refused : " It is for those Beings to come to me, not for me to go to them."

' What was in his mind in so lofty an utterance we could not explain to ourselves and we dared not ask him.'

But the saying of Plotinus was not a lofty utterance, nor was there any arrogance in it; he was simply stating a fact of his own experience in writing his *Enneads* and, perhaps, in the conduct of his life.

Here is a short passage from Ennead I, 6 . . . [*Plotinus* : Creuzer, Oxford 1835, which has a Latin Version], translated with the help of Stephen MacKenna :

> ' But how can you see into a virtuous soul and know its loveliness?
> ' Withdraw into yourself and look. And if you do not find yourself beautiful yet, act as does the creator of a statue that is to be made beautiful : he cuts away here, he smoothes there, he makes this line lighter, this other purer, until a lovely face has grown upon his work . . .
> ' When you know that you have become this perfect work, when you are self-gathered in the purity of your being, nothing now remaining that can shatter that inner unity, nothing from without clinging to the authentic man, when you find yourself wholly true to your essential nature, wholly that only veritable Light . . . strain and see.

'This is the only eye that sees the mighty Beauty. If the eye that adventures the vision be dimmed by vice, impure or weak, and unable in its cowardly blenching to see the uttermost brightness, then it sees nothing even though another point to what lies plain to sight before it. To any vision must be brought an eye adapted to what is to be seen, and having some likeness to it. Never did eye see the sun unless it had first become sunlike, and never can the soul have vision of the First Beauty unless itself be beautiful.'

When we read or (better) hear the poetry of Blake or Hopkins or the ' poetry ' of Plotinus, we are not concerned with Blake or Hopkins or Plotinus. They are instruments to be played on, and the music belongs to us. We are concerned with its effect upon ourselves. And if we are asked what the effect is, we can only say that ' something happens,' something that approximates to the experience of Browning, when he knew Christ named his name, or of Richard Rolle when he saw the Cross swaying in the stone, or of Newman when he heard the Angel.

IV

INTUITION

IV

INTUITION

WE come at length to the norm, of which Vision and the Spiritual Imperative are more or less supernormal forms : Intuition.

I

In Scholastic Philosophy, Intuition is regarded as the immediate knowledge ascribed to angelic and spiritual beings, with whom Vision and knowledge are identical. In Modern Philosophy, Intuition may be defined as the ' immediate apprehension of an object by the mind without the intervention of any reasoning process.' [1] I would remind the reader that Blake says that Invention, Identity and Melody are the Objects of Intuition.

Plotinus, whose writings I began to study because Dr Edward Caird in his *Evolution of Theology in the Greek Philosophers* (1904) calls him ' the Mystic *par excellence,*' [2] has three phases or images of the Divine-Soul, or, as we should call them, three stages of Cognition. The highest is the intellective-soul or intuitive, intellectual or intelligent soul or the intellectual-principle of the soul.[3]

[1] S.O.E.D., p. 1037.　　　　[2] Vol. II, p. 211.
[3] His account of the three stages is in *Ennead* VI, 7, 2.

Blake insists that all real knowledge is intuitive. He goes so far as to say that education is a great sin. Connected with this view of knowledge is his belief in the significance of all mundane forms : they are symbols of spiritual ideas revealed to the inspired man. This is Plotinus's highest stage of cognition, and he makes it clear that there are three stages, and that the ' education ' of the other stages is necessary.

As Plotinus with his dialectical conception corresponds in his cognition at its highest degree of certainty to Spinoza's knowledge of the third kind or *scientia intuitiva*, I will take a hint from Thomas Whittaker [1] and give Spinoza's mathematical conception of the three stages as the easier.

' From what has been already said, it clearly appears that we perceive many things and form universal ideas :

1. From individual things, represented by the senses to us in a mutilated and confused manner and without order to the intellect. These perceptions I have therefore been in the habit of calling knowledge from vague experience.

2. From signs; as, for example, when we hear or read certain words, we recollect things and form ideas of them similar to them, through which ideas we imagine things. These two ways of looking at things I will hereafter call knowledge of the first kind, opinion or imagination.

3. From our possessing common notions and adequate ideas of the properties of things. This I shall call reason and knowledge of the second kind.

[1] The Neo-Platonists, p. 109.

' Besides these two kinds of knowledge, there is a third, as I shall hereafter show, which we shall call intuitive science. This kind of knowing advances from an adequate idea of the formal essence of certain attributes of God to the adequate knowledge of the essence of things. All this I will explain by one example. Let there be three numbers given through which it is required to discover a fourth, which shall be to the third as the second is to the first. A merchant does not hesitate to multiply the second and third together and divide the product by the first, either because he has not yet forgotten the things which he heard without any demonstration from his schoolmaster, or because he has seen the truth of the rule with the more simple numbers, or because from the 19th Prop. in the 7th book of Euclid he understands the common property of all proportionals.

' But with the simplest numbers there is no need of all this. If the numbers 1, 2, 3, for instance be given, every one can see that the fourth proportional is 6 much more clearly than by any demonstration, because from the ratio in which we see by one intuition that the first stands to the second, we conclude the fourth.' [1]

Spinoza's 43rd Prop. is :—' *He who has a true idea knows at the same time that he has a true idea, nor can he doubt the truth of the thing.*'

' Every one can see,' says Spinoza. Spinoza's example of the simplest numbers is a self-evident

[1] Benedict de Spinoza (originally Baruch de Spinoza) was born at Amsterdam on Nov. 24th, 1632. He died on Feb. 21st, 1677. His *Ethic* was not published until after his death. The quotations are from the translation of W. Hale White, revised by Amelia Stirling, 2nd Ed. (T. Fisher Unwin), 1894 : Ethic II, Prop. 40, Schol. 2.

example. All intuitive knowledge is self-evident to the percipient. The psychological explanation is that the knowledge is subjective, and the explanation has this truth : that the intuition is conditioned by the receptivity of the person who receives it. Spinoza's saying, ' This kind of knowing advances from an adequate idea of the formal essence of certain attributes of God to the adequate knowledge of the essence of things ' may be transferred to other areas of education and experience. Marshal Foch said that the plan of the battle of July 18th, 1918, ' came ' to him. But it would not have come to anyone. He had an adequate idea of strategy and tactics. His military education and experience qualified him to be a receptive person. Nevertheless, the plan ' came ' to him. The preparation for the intuition of the ratio 1 to 2 passes unnoticed. The preparation for the ' coming ' of the plan is obvious. And when Marshal Foch had the idea of the plan, he knew, by a parallel intuition, that it was a true plan, and he waited for the event to re-inforce the truth of the idea, or, rather, to demonstrate to others the truth. He himself had the true idea and knew at the same time that it was a true idea.

The intuition of his plan came to Foch in the course of his ordinary avocation. I suppose the plan would be called an act of the empirical consciousness.

It is the general consciousness of which Eckhart [1] speaks : ' The intuitive, higher knowledge is timeless and spaceless, without here and now.'

[1] Quoted from *Mysticism East and West* by Rudolf Otto, p. 35. The German Meister Eckhart lived from 1250 to 1327. His great speculative work is *Opus tripartitum*.

Rudolf Otto's book, from which I have quoted this passage, is an attempt to ' penetrate the nature of that strange spiritual phenomenon which we call mysticism by comparing the two principal classic types of Eastern and Western mystical experience.' He compares the Indian Śankara and the German Meister Eckart. He finds ' an astonishing conformity in the deepest impulses of human spiritual experience, which—because it is almost entirely independent of race, clime and age—points to an ultimate inward similarity of the human spirit, and justifies us in speaking of a uniform nature of mysticism. But we are immediately confronted with the equally important task of showing the possibilities of manifold singularities occurring within this uniform nature, and thereby of meeting the erroneous assumption that mysticism is " one and ever the same." '

Otto says that a ' fundamental *intuitus mysticus* lies at the basis of the teaching both of Eckhart and Śankara, and is the real source of their strange assertions and deep pathos.' The intuition is a first-hand and immediate fact and possession of the intuitive mind.

The forms that Eckhart uses were more cloaks and disguises to his thought than explanations of it.

This may be true generally of intuitive persons, especially when their intuitions concern conduct or the tasks they undertake. S. Angus [1] says that ' throughout the whole history of Greek thought there

[1] *The Mystery Religions and Christianity* (1925), p. 13. I would commend this book to students for exposition of the vital way in which Christianity is superior to the Mystery Religions. See especially for this purpose p. 309 onwards.

ran two concurrent and often conflicting tendencies, the " scientific " and the " mystical," the Olympian and the Dionysian, the philosophical and the intuitional.'

These tendencies persist. Men may be divided into two classes : the Wise, those who deliberate and act on principle; and the Fools, those who follow their intuitions. The Wise are justified in common opinion; they are still the Olympians. But even they are sometimes ' jumped ' into acting as Fools act, ' on the spur of the moment,' when they are in a tight place and have no time to deliberate. The Fools wait for the event to justify their intuitive decisions. They may have their natural misgivings while they are waiting, but at the moment of decision they have no doubt at all. Eckhart notices the aperçu-nature (to use Goethe's phrase) of the deeper knowledge realising itself in individual acts of the empirical consciousness.

Intuition is very swift, and in an incredibly short space of time may cover a large field. Eckhart says it is timeless and spaceless. A flash of lightning (*velut coruscatione perstringeris*) is Augustine's image.

The Fools are usually averse from admitting that they act on intuition—I mean the confirmed fools, those who make a habit of trusting their intuitions. They often borrow their forms of explanation from the Wise and elaborate into reason the acts that were not the result of reasoning.

I suppose we must still look to the Wise, the philosophical, the scientific for the due ordering of political

and commercial and even domestic life. Lord
Palmerston was a Fool, and he was not altogether a
failure, but we must continue to trust the reasoning
animals, in spite of Keyserling's *dictum* that ' the
post-war leaders far surpass the pre-war leaders in
intuition and consequently in general mental ability.' [1]

Before we return to Eckhart for a particular purpose,
I will make further use of Otto's book to distinguish
between the ' inward ' and the ' outward ' way of
intuition. In Plotinus both types intermingle. Here
is the first type from a passage in the *Sixth Ennead* :

' Often when I awake from the slumber of the body,
and step out of the outward world in order to turn
in upon myself, I behold a wonderful beauty. Then
I believe unshakeably that I belong to a better world;
most glorious life works strongly in me and I am one
with the Godhead. Transferred into this I have
reached that vital energy and have raised myself above
all intellectual things. When I climb down from this
rest in the lap of the Godhead to intellectual under-
standing I ask myself how there can possibly be a
sinking back out of that condition.'

For the other type take the following extract from
the *Fifth Ennead* :

' They see all not in process of becoming but in
Being, and they see themselves in the other. Each
Being contains within itself the whole intelligible
world. Therefore all is everywhere. Each is there
all and all is each.'

The particular purpose for which I wish to return
to Eckhart is to draw the reader's attention to some

[1] *The World in the Making*, p. 185.

passages, which have the quality of a poet's utterances
rather than of a preacher's. The impression of them
is strangely like the impression of Blake's poetry, and
they seem to me to be spontaneous in expression, not
worked over at all with the aid of doctoral didacticism
or anything else.

' The wheel revolving out of itself ' (for God or the
Godhead)

' The stream flowing into itself '

' God flourishing and growing in the ground of the
soul ' [1]

' Defect means lack of being.'

' God is the only value.'

' It is as when a man pours water into a clean vessel and
lets it stand, and, then, if he holds his face over it he sees
his face at the bottom as it is in itself '

(The ' spiritual understanding ' here is the sight of the
man really looking at himself in the clear calm water. Or,
to take a looking-glass and a man shaving himself before
it: as a rule he is preoccupied by the process of shaving,
but once in a hundred times he may see his own face as
it is in itself.).

' To be *installed* in God '

' Becoming one and (at the same time) becoming
nothing ' (If you enter into the oneness of life you become
free from accident.)

' Gather in contemplation and give out in love.'

' I am that I am (*Sum qui sum*) . . . a boiling up and
pouring out of itself in itself, scalding and melting and
bubbling itself within itself, light penetrating light, itself
whole penetrating the whole self . . . Life is a gushing
up . . . pouring any part of itself into any other part,
before it runs forth and bubbles over without.'

' Like a horse turned loose into a lush meadow giving
vent to his horse-nature by galloping full-tilt about the
field.'

' He loves and creates. Work is His nature, His being,
His life, His happiness.'

The whole of the strange sermon called ' The
Soul's Rage.'

[1] *cf.* Julian of Norwich : ' I am Ground of thy beseeching ' (the com-
plementary aspect), *op cit.*, p. 84.

Eckhart has been described as the 'first great Gothic figure,[1] but there co-exist in him a conception of the *homo nobilis* [2] and humility. To him humility is the threshold virtue of the house of life.

I cannot resist the temptation to speak again of intuition and conduct. On what condition or basis can a man trust the suggestions that come into his mind? How can he be sure that the suggestions are good and true? Spinoza would say: By the parallel intuition of the truth. Julian of Norwich would say: By comparing them with the teaching of Holy Church. Henry Suso says: 'What is absolute experience will harmonize with the teaching of Holy Writ.'[3] But a man may give way to a weakening afterthought, whereby he is led to doubt the parallel intuition. Or, he may have no real access to any authoritative teaching. What then? I have a theory that subjection to events [4] is the condition. I have seen this hinted at by Plotinus and St. Augustine, but the theory does not proceed from them.

Resentment of events is a kind of blindness or death of the mind, and, in Wordsworth's word, 'hoodwinks' the intuitions.

Subjection to events is more than acquiescence, as the word implies. The danger is that subjection to events may degenerate into subjection to persons. Mutual love or friendship may eliminate the danger. 'God is the only value,' but God is the same value to

[1] Rudolf Otto: *op. cit.,* p. 181.
[2] What would the whole world profit a man if he were not more than it?
[3] *The Life of the Blessed Henry Suso,* p. 240.
[4] See also the Pope's verdict on Pompilia's intuition (p. 22).

those who love one another, and the intuitions of the
one may be freely and spontaneously accepted and
assimilated by the other.

Many men have an area of experience in which
they have learned to trust their intuitions. They are
usually highly skilled and have spent a common life
in their searches or researches.

The ordinary man knows the worth of intuitions.
Six or seven years ago I travelled by train from Liver-
pool to Euston, when for the whole journey there was
only one other occupant of the compartment. This
man described to me a strange accident that had hap-
pened to him, and, beginning from this mishap, he
poured out, in a continuous stream, details of his
past life. I felt it was a help to him to unburden
himself, but I wondered why, in the delicate care of
God, I should be the particular person to share his
confidences. At length he suddenly exclaimed:
' What a different man I should have been, if I had
only obeyed the suggestions that God put into my
mind from time to time ! '

The English are peculiarly gifted with this faculty
of intuition.

' What is it that is incomprehensible about these
islanders? It is the particular adjustment of their
psyche—the only one of its kind in Europe. With
them the emphasis lies not on the conscious but on
the unconscious.

' It is not intelligence but instinct—rising at its
highest to intuition—which determines the course of
their lives . . . When Field-Marshal Roberts died,
one obituary contained the following appraisal:

Roberts had two great virtues : first, his instinct;
second, his belief in his instinct.[1]

‘ And precisely because of his lack of intellectuality,
the Englishman far outranks any other European in
his ability to establish direct contact with the human
element in others. He is the man who, first and last,
sees into and understands his fellow-man. He does
this even with those whom he is actually oppressing.
He never behaves as though they were not human
beings; he is always ready to recognize, as a funda-
mental human right, their particular character; and
he never awakens in others the feeling that to him
the thing matters more than the person [2] . . .

‘ But what happens when this psychological con-
formation must serve to express a profound person-
ality ? In that case something altogether extra-
ordinary ensues . . . Nowhere can fine and profound
souls be found in equal numbers. Thus it happens
that England is the one modern country which
instinctively understands happiness as a spiritual
quality . . . Yet, sometimes . . . . we encounter a soul
endowed with natural depth, and then its happiness is
like the happiness of the blest. Then it means being
anchored in that serenity which out of its strength
can accept in joy all the world’s pain. Then it means
being lifted for ever beyond the plane of the tragic.’

[1] *Europe.* ‘ Das Spektrum Europas ’ by Hermann Keyserling. Trans.
by Maurice Samuel (Cape, 1928), p. 19. *cf.* ‘ The remarkable thing
about Burne-Jones, and this applies to his technical performance, as in
drawing, as well as to his conceptions, was the high artistic level he
reached by an inner impulse, and neither by intellectual grasp of form
nor truth of the visual impression. When we classify artists we are apt
to forget this, peculiarly English, possibility.’ Art Critic of *The Times,*
June 17, 1933, on the Burne-Jones Centenary Exhibition at the Tate
Gallery.

[2] *op. cit.,* p. 27.

For the purpose of analysis I have accented, and accented strongly, Intuition, and I shall continue to accent it. But I wish also to stress the need of preparation for the intuition. Man is noble in reason; his gift must be perfected. He is infinite in faculty; his faculty must not rust in disuse. In form and moving he is express and admirable; he must keep up his form and not waddle through life. It is only in the exercise of all these that he can hope to act like the messenger of God and apprehend faultlessly the Divine command. Then he becomes, on the one hand, the glory of the world, the living man in action; and, on the other hand, the paragon of animals, the contemplative, who in the stillness of his spirit sees God for what He is.

II

Intuition, then, in any of its forms, is a mode of apprehension different from the reasoning process. It may concern various areas of experience, but when the intuitive mind is directed towards the things of God ($\tau \grave{a} \ \tau o \hat{v} \ \theta \epsilon o \hat{v}$ [1]), intuition is called mystical intuition and the knowledge so possessed, mystical knowledge.

The poetic mind is also an intuitive mind and poetic knowledge is intuitive knowledge. The ' good ' of the poetic experience ' goes ' for the poet through his care to find words for it, but the hearing of his poetry may engender in others a similar experience to his own.

[1] St Mark, 8, 33.

What, then, is the relation between the poet and the mystic, and between the poetic experience and the ' mystical experience,' traditionally so called ? I quote from Henri Bremond [1] :

' Le poète pur n'exista jamais; l'expérience poétique pure est un mythe. Un grand poète peut être aussi un homme pieux, voire un contemplatif authentique. Saint Augustin par example, ou l'auteur de l'*Imitation*. Mais de ceux-ci même, l'activité poétique, dégagée par un effort d'analyse et isolée des mille activités qui l'accompagnent, la bloquent, la secondent et la gênent tour à tour, n'est un acte formel ni d'amour ni même de foi. Rien de proprement religieux, rien de méritoire. Je ne parle bien entendu que des pages des *Confessions* qui égalent par leur magie verbale les plus beaux vers de Virgile. Plus ces pages sont poétiquement parfaite, moins elles sont prière, et moins elles sont prière, plus elles sont génératrices de prière. Et cela directement, automatiquement, pour ainsi dire, non à la manière des sermons ou des effusions pieuses qui restent prose. Car il ne s'agit pas, encore une fois, des idées que présente le poète, ou des sentiments qu'il éveille; il s'agit du mouvement qu'il imprime au centre de nos âmes, déclenchant par là tout un mécanisme psychologique dont les ressorts n'ont plus besoin que d'une motion surnaturelle pour s'adapter aux activités propres, pour servir les fins spéciales de la vraie prière . . . . '

The summary of Henri Bremond's brilliant and penetrating thesis is :

' 1° Il y a une autre pensée que la pensée abstraite

[1] *op. cit.*, 218, 219, 220, 221.

et discursive; une autre connaissance que la connais-
sance conceptuelle et rationelle; 2° ni la connaissance
réelle, ni la rationelle, lesquelles, d'ailleurs, ne
se développent pas l'une sans l'autre, ne s'achèvent
sans impliquer l'exercice des facultés que met
divinement en œuvre la vie mystique.   D'où
l'excellence, et tout ensemble l'imperfection essenti-
elle de l'expérience poétique : pierre d'attente d'une
expérience plus haute, qu'elle appelle, en quelque
sorte, mais où d'elle-même elle ne saurait conduire,
qu'elle empêcherait plutôt.'

I ask the reader to compare these passages with
what I have tried to say in the previous pages.

V

THE TRADITIONAL VIEW OF MYSTICISM

V

THE TRADITIONAL VIEW OF MYSTICISM

TRADITIONALLY, mysticism is a way of praying, and the ' mystical experience ' is the intuitive apprehension of God or the intuition of God as present.[1]

Taking a parallel from poetry, one may define poetry as a way of saying. Poetry, however, is not any way of saying, but *a* way, and intuition is essential to poetry.[2] So, mysticism is not any way of praying, but *a* way, and the fundamental mystical phenomenon is an intuition. There is no question at all of a rational or notional illumination. The ' mystical experience ' is not a revelation.

The tradition goes back to the original use of the word ' mystic '[3] among the Greeks and forward among Christians to the present day, without regard to ' religious differences.'

I

As my first salient spiritual experience came in listening to a poem, I begin from the side of the poets.

Recall the passage quoted from Abbé Bremond's

[1] *cf.* Bremond, *op. cit.,* p. 143.

[2] See Blake (*passim*); Camb. Hist. of Eng. Lit., xii, p. 72; *The Fountain* by Charles Morgan, p. 112; Preface to *Halfway House* by Edmund Blunden.

[3] ' Mystic ' is the Gk. μύστης and ' mystical ' the Gk. μυστικός. The abstract term, ' mysticism,' came much later, probably in 1763.

book. He says that the poet *qua* poet is neither moral nor pious; that ' the more poetically perfect his pages are, the further they are from prayer; and the further they are from prayer, the more productive they are of prayer.' Might we not say, the more they lead the listeners to praying? We are not here concerned with the poet's ideas or with the sentiments he awakes; ' we are concerned with the movement which he imprints on the centre of our souls,' and it is this movement which may serve the special ends of true prayer.

My experience, then, in listening to the *Ancient Mariner,* was, in Abbé Bremond's view, an experience of prayer. Coleridge [1] had anticipated Bremond. After hearing Wordsworth read the *Prelude* he wrote a poem on the effect of listening to it, which ends :

> Scarce conscious, and yet conscious of its close
> I sate, my being blended in one thought
> (Thought was it? or aspiration? or resolve?)
> Absorbed, yet hanging still upon the sound—
> And when I rose, I found myself in prayer.

Emerson meant the same when he speaks of the effect upon him of

> Revisit'st thus the glimpses of the moon.

My father said he sat back and ' tasted ' it. But it was the ' relish ' (to use Gerard Hopkins's word) of prayer.

When I felt a great amazement at Hotspur's dying speech :

> But thought's the slave of life, and life's time's fool;
> And time, that takes survey of all the world,
> Must have a stop—

I was really praying.

[1] *To William Wordsworth.*

A. E. Housman says [1] : ' But in these six simple words of Milton :—

> Nymphs and shepherds, dance no more—

what is it that can draw tears, as I know it can, to the eyes of more readers than one? What in the world is there to cry about? Why have the mere words the physical effect of pathos when the sense of the passage is blithe and gay? I can only say, because they are poetry, and find their way to something in man which is obscure and latent, something older than the present organisation of his nature . . .'

Would not Bremond say that the six words started the psychological mechanism of prayer? It sounds a flat account after Prof. Housman's, but the last word redeems it, for ' prayer ' dilates the closet to the world's dimensions.

Shakespeare can give more moments of this kind than any other poet. He can *sustain* the moment. *Twelfth Night* always produces in me a Kingdom of Heaven feeling, as if it were a play of children, some of them bent on a mischievous trick to ' floor ' an interfering grown-up. Perhaps the ' poetic experience ' of the poet was the same, for he turns sadly at the end to grown-up life :

> When that I was and a little tiny boy
>   With hey, ho, the wind and the rain;
> A foolish thing was but a toy,
>   For the rain it raineth every day.
>
> But when I came to man's estate . . .

[1] *The Name and Nature of Poetry*, p. 46.

Why is *Hamlet* a play of love?   What is there in

> Go, bid the soldiers shoot

that sounds like the trump of God?
And the *Tempest?*

> Full fathom five thy father lies;
>   Of his bones are coral made;
> Those are pearls which were his eyes;
>   Nothing of him that doth fade,
> But doth suffer a sea-change
> Into something rich and strange . . .

I heard my father laugh in a kind of ecstasy over
that. What is there to laugh about? Yet his laugh-
ter was a kind of prayer.

Keats can give such moments. I said to a friend
of mine, ' Keats first wrote : " A thing of beauty is a
constant joy " '—just to hear what he would say,
adding : ' Isn't that slightly truer than " A thing of
beauty is a joy for ever " ? '

He said, ' But the other is authentic—the current
passes.'

Or,

> O magic sleep! O comfortable bird! [1]

> Love's standard on the battlements of song [2]

> Down whose green back the short-lived foam all hoar
> Bursts gradual with a wayward indolence [3]

> Then felt I like some watcher of the skies
>   When a new planet swims into his ken;
> Or like stout Cortez when with eagle eyes
>   He stared at the Pacific—and all his men
> Look'd at each other with a mild surmise—
>   Silent upon a peak in Darien. [4]

Tennyson, with four words—

> O that 'twere possible . . . [5]

[1] *Endymion.*   [2] *Ibid.*   [3] *Ibid.*
[4] *On first looking into Chapman's Homer.*
[5] *Maud.*

A. E. Housman—

> The ship of sunrise burning
> Strands upon the eastern rims.[1]

> The cuckoo shouts all day at nothing
> In leafy dells alone.[2]

T. S. Eliot, sometimes—

> Who is the third who walks always beside you? [3]

C. H. Sorley—

> We shall all come tumbling down
> To our old wrinkled red-capped town.[4]

But all listeners are not the same. I repeated Blake's stanza,

> Though thou art worshipp'd by the names divine
> Of Jesus and Jehovah, thou art still
> The Son of Morn in weary night's decline,
> The lost traveller's dream under the hill

to one friend, and he said, ' It makes one want to be the lost traveller; ' and to another, and he looked at me with hostility, as if he had just dodged a missile that I had flung at him. Many people are bored, even outraged, by poetry. Some who like Shakespeare's plays dislike the poetry in them, and, if they quote from Shakespeare, never, by any chance, quote a poetical passage.

If poetry is to move to praying, it can only be by the exercise of the same faculty (or, gift) in the listener as went to the making of the poem. The fruit of intuition is only to be tasted by the intuitive.[5] And the praying, says Bremond, may lead on to the mystical experience, of which the poet, by his very poetic activity has robbed himself.

[1] *A Shropshire Lad.*   [2] *Last Poems.*   [3] *The Waste Land.*
[4] C. H. Sorley: *Marlborough and Other Poems,* XXXVI.
[5] *cf. Halfway House* by Edmund Blunden, p. 83, and *The Life of the Blessed Henry Suso,* p. 238.

Even if one cannot accept Bremond's account of the poetic activity and its effects, one must accept ' praying ' as covering the whole spiritual process, if one is to understand the traditional view of mysticism.

I have described the process in my own case from the first disturbing and exhilarating experience, through the disciplines and joys and delicately careful adjustments to some sort of quiet climax.   The reader will notice that at one point I was told ' not to pray ' and that I considered it as a discharge from warfare, that is to say, from an agony that I was no longer capable of enduring.   This sense of agony had come upon me in 1916 when I faced the fact that my son might be killed and I deliberately contended with God and offered myself in his place.   I thought he was too young to die.   I had not then really perceived, though I was convinced I had, that some maidens and youths as well as some little children and girls and boys may make so rapid a progress that they become ' fit,' as some athletes with an aptitude for a game qualify themselves for the highest kind of play in a very short time.

I was told not to say prayers.   That was in my period of listening.

Then came the belief in the imperceptible—I cannot find any other word—and the accompanying recognition of God in very little things.   There was another mark of release and that was the expectation of good, the feeling of ' what comes next.' [1]   ' Wait and see ' became a counsel of joyous expectancy. Even when untoward, or, apparently untoward, things

[1] *cf. The Dream* by John Masefield : ' Save the all-living joy of what comes next.'

happened, I used to think, ' Wait and see. This un-
toward thing will turn out to be part of a beautiful
scheme.'

You have seen the place of Vision in this process.
Vision came, because I needed Vision—clear, unmis-
takable (like an act contrasted with a tale)—and the
first vision came when I knelt to pray and thought I
needed nothing at all.

Many of the great ones have begun with Vision :
St. Paul, St. Catherine of Genoa, Ramon Lull
(pulled up in his tracks) and others. St. Paul quoted
his vision as evidence of the power of God to raise
the dead.[1] Did he mean only that he himself had seen
the risen Lord, or did he mean also that he himself
had been raised from the dead—lifted out of death
into life ?

Vision, however, may come at any time or not at
all. What I wish to emphasize now is that this ex-
perience from first to last was, in the proper sense of
the term, an experience of praying.

Does there come a point in praying when no
striving or learning will avail ? We have seen the
consensus of opinion that without something else a
verse-maker cannot become a poet. The first condition
of poetry is intuition. Is there a point at which
intuition enters for praying ? For intuition is really
an abandonment in faith. Without this abandon-
ment in faith there cannot be any poetic experience.
A similar abandonment in faith is necessary for the
' mystical experience.'

The poet sings. His release into poetry is extra-

[1] Acts xxvi, 8.

ordinarily happy. But when he has sung, or, even as he sings, virtue dies out of him, the poetic experience is dissipated, the good goes; he ' never wants to look at the thing again.' He waits for the next spark from heaven to fall, but the next spark will die in just the same way, when his poetic activity is over.

But the mystic is silent. If he speaks, it is out of the incredibly intense quickening which precedes the stillness. He speaks at great risk to himself. To others he may seem to be talking nonsense; he is straining language beyond its capacity; and the ordinary hearer cannot fathom what he means. The mystical experience itself is ineffable, and, because it has this quality, it cannot be dissipated, like the poetic experience.

The contemplative is moved to action. What he gathers in contemplation he gives out in love. The ministry of an authentic contemplative,[1] cleric or lay, man or woman, learned or unlearned, has a divine touch. It is like bread to the hungry, water to the thirsty, sleep to the anguished mind and body :

> Sleep that knits up the ravell'd sleave of care,
> The death of each day's life, sore labour's bath,
> Balm of hurt minds, great nature's second course,
> Chief nourisher in life's feast . . . [2]

like the joyous echoes of his youth to the old and weary :

> But, best of all, if after
>   The years that lie behind him,
> The poet hears the laughter
>   Of the boy who comes to find him—
> The boy he was, heedless of life's disdain—
> To heal him of his pain.

[1] See *The Bugler's First Communion* and *Felix Rendal* by G. M. Hopkins.
[2] Macbeth, Act II, Sc. II, 38*ff*.

II

Dom Cuthbert Butler wrote his book, *Western Mysticism*,[1] on a kind of challenge to clear up the muddle and to tell us what Mysticism is and what qualifies for a mystic. He says that the least that will qualify a man or a woman to be called a mystic is ' the prayer of loving attention—nothing less than it is mystical. The will heaves itself up blindly and bluntly to God and the mind works in a way outside the ordinary laws of phenomenal psychology.' I wonder if this description of a ' prayer of loving attention ' does clear up the muddle. By ' blindly and bluntly ' he may be seeking to indicate the helplessness which the spiritual imperative is sometimes meant to relieve, or the self-abandonment in obedience to the Will of a Power outside and greater than themselves which is characteristic alike of the strong and sensible and of those who are conscious of their own weakness and indecisiveness. But the attention, as befits the word, must be wide-awake and sharp. The apprehension is intuitive, not rational. Psychology must take into account intuitions, or it cannot pretend to be ' the science which investigates behaviour in general, from the point of view of its mental implications.' [2]

Dom Butler also desires that the term mystical ' should be restricted to that experimental perception of God, however expressed, that is the real claim of mystics in their higher states of contemplation and

[1] *Western Mysticism* by Dom Cuthbert Butler, 1927 Ed. ' Afterthoughts,' pp. lxxxiv and lxxxv. Dom Butler died on Easter Day 1934. He was formerly Abbot of Downside.
[2] *An Introduction to Psychology* by F. Aveling, p. 174.

union—the assertion on the validity of which depends the religious and philosophical importance of mysticism, properly so-called.'

' Above all ' he says ' it is greatly to be desired that the use of the words " mysticism," " mystical " be strictly confined to this religious and philosophical meaning.'

Dom Butler has some noble words at the end of his book.[1] He speaks of the mystical element of will and emotion and personal religious experience as an essential element of religion, and the element of the service to others as another essential element . . . . ' In regard to the mystical element itself, it is not to be cultivated as a thing apart from the everyday duties of life . . . Nor are these things the preserve of the intellectual and the educated, or of any spiritually leisured class; they are open to all—to the poor and unlettered and to the lowly workers, who spend their lives in alternation between the conscientious performance of their daily round of humble duties and the regular recourse to God in affective prayer and rudimentary contemplation.'

In his Afterthoughts, from which I have already quoted, Dom Butler would so restrict ' mysticism ' and ' mystical ' as to leave out all who have not attained to the ' higher states of contemplation and union.' Is then the mystical element an essential element of religion ? Père de Maumigny, who died

---

[1] *Western Mysticism*, p. 324. Contrast: On n'a jamais cité un seul auteur qui ait dit avant le père Poulain : *La connaissance expérimentale de Dieu est une perception directe de l'Être divin lui-même.* (Saudreau, *op. cit.*, p. 321). Saudreau also says that ' affective prayer ' is not a mystical experience.

in 1918, adhered [1] firmly to the doctrine that con-
templation is an extraordinary kind of prayer,
demanding a special vocation, and exhorted all those
who were not favoured with this special vocation not
to lose courage but to persevere generously in the
common way, in which they will never get beyond
meditation, believing that this path will lead them
to sanctity. Père Poulain is on the same side, but is
vigorously refuted by Canon Auguste Saudreau in
L'État Mystique.

The ideal (if one may call it) of the contemplative
is variously described as the prayer of passive union,
the life of conscious union with God, the Beatific
Vision, or, by the Brabant John Ruysbroeck, as the
superessential life. St. Teresa [2] speaks of it as the
spiritual marriage, thereby giving rise to the entirely
erroneous impression that mysticism is erotic mysti-
cism. St. John of the Cross [3] reserves the Beatific
Vision for the life of the world to come :—' For this
loving obscure knowledge, which is faith, serves in a
manner in this life as means of the divine union, as
the light of glory hereafter serves for the beatific
vision.'

St. John of the Cross, in the preface to Stanza xix
of his *Spiritual Canticle* writes of the effect of this
experience : ' Of a truth the soul is now lost to all
things and gained only to love, and the mind is no
longer occupied with anything else. It is, therefore,
deficient in what concerns the active life and other

[1] *Pratique de l'oraison mentale, passim.*
[2] *The Interior Castle.*
[3] *The Ascent of Mount Carmel,* pp. 199, 200. In this he seems to agree
with St Augustine : ' Contemplation is only begun in this life, to be
perfected in the next ' (*Tract. in Joan.* cxxiv, 5).

external duties, that it may apply itself in earnest to the one thing which the Bridegroom has pronounced necessary . . .' [1]

On the other hand, Ruysbroeck, both in his *Adornment of the Spiritual Marriage* and in his *Sparkling Stone* insists on fruition [2] : ' The man who is sent down by God from these heights (*i.e.*, the superessential life) into the world is full of truth and rich in all virtues. He possesses a rich and generous ground, which is set in the richness of God; and therefore *he must always spend himself on those who are in need of him*.[3] He is a living and willing instrument of God, with which God works whatsoever He will and howsoever He will. And he remains ready to do in the virtues all that God commands, and strong and courageous in suffering all that God allows to befall him. And by this he possesses an universal life, for he is ready alike for contemplation and for action, and is perfect in both of them. And none can have this universal life save the God-seeing man.' [4]

III

For the attainment of the ideal, there is a definite technique which I have called the Scheme of Prayer.

One finds the technique developed most methodically among Latin Christians. The German Eckhart mentions the method, but he is not a follower of it

[1] This quotation is from Dom Butler's book.

[2] So does St Teresa (*opus cit.*), Seventh Mansion (c.3).

[3] Italics mine.

[4] This is also the view of Richard de St Victor (col. 1216, Vol. cxcxi of Migne, Paris, 1880).

in any technical sense. He was a man of great spiritual independence and was excommunicated after his death on the strange charge that he had revealed the secrets of the priesthood to the laity. Roman Catholic writers hardly mention him. Eckhart's disciple, the Swiss Suso, in the Prologue prefixed to his Life, claims that his book ' teaches the orderly and proper course by which a man may attain to the unalloyed truth of a blessed and perfect life,' but it is difficult to recognise the method in his course. Neither are the acknowledged English Mystics of the fourteenth century—the flowering time of English Mysticism— Richard Rolle, Walter Hilton and Dame Julian, strict followers of the method. The English temperament differs from the Latin, and the English Mystics are especially marked by their devotion to the Holy Name of Jesus, and by ' Name ' they mean all that Christians mean when they say, ' Hallowed be Thy Name.' Julian says : ' for where Jesus appeareth, the Blessed Trinity is understood, for my sight.'

The technique is clear enough. The stages [1] are *Via Purgativa, Via Illuminativa* and *Via Unitiva*.[2]

The beginner recognizes the Divine Reality and turns away from the world of unreality.[3] He deliberately concentrates himself upon God or a religious idea, and his attention is therefore averted from the outward world. The aversion from the outer world is in the beginner more strongly marked than his

[1] It is a mistake to call these stages *The Mystic Way*. The mystic is the initiate, who has reached the *Via Illuminativa* and begins to be a contemplative.

[2] St. Augustine has seven stages : 5th, *tranquilitas;* 6th, *ingressio;* 7th, *contemplatio.*

[3] See *Prayer* by Friedrich Heiler, p. 283.

conversion to God. If one compares the lectures on
Conversion in William James's *Varieties of Religious
Experience* with the remarks on beginners by Suso
and St. John of the Cross, one sees that William
James, not being pre-occupied with the matter of
technique, discusses conversion in a broader sense
than we ought to use, if there is to be any clear con-
ception of the Scheme as defined by the professed
contemplatives.

God does indeed allure beginners [1] by a foretaste
of the Divine Consolations, but the life of Union is
not attained except through perseverance.

Purgation [2] really begins when the soul has retired
within the barriers, in order to repress the senses and
reflect upon God.

St. John of the Cross [3] draws a clear distinction
between meditation and contemplation. Meditation
is for him who is treading the way of purgation :

' In order to have a better knowledge of the state
of beginners we must keep in mind that it is one of
meditation and of acts of reflection. It is necessary
to furnish the soul in this state with matter for medi-
tation, that it may make reflections and interior acts,
and avail itself of the sensible heat and fervour, for
this is necessary in order to accustom the senses and
desires to good things, that being satisfied with the
·sweetness thereof they may be detached from the
world.'

Meditation demands matter—images such as may

[1] Suso, p. 19.

[2] Contrast Eckhart : ' the works of the *via purgativa* can only be per-
formed when the Eternal has been found and attained.' Rudolf Otto,
op. cit., p. 29.

[3] *The Living Flame*, iii.

be gazed upon in a chapel, the Crucifix, the Stations, the Judge and the Angels; and it avails itself of sensible spiritual heat and fervour.

Then follows, according to St John of the Cross, the Dark Night of the Sense. This is not to be regarded as a set-back, but as an inevitable condition, through which the soul has to pass. ' Souls in this state are not to be forced to meditate or to apply themselves to discursive reflections laboriously effected.'

As the soul emerges from this Dark Night, it enters on the Illuminative Way. The subject begins to be a mystic. Contemplation, not merely meditation, is necessary to the mystic.

' All contemplatives, perfect and imperfect, agree in this, which is it that distinguisheth their way from other ways, that they immediately, without the means of images or creatures, apply themselves to God, or to seek union with Him by the powers of the soul, but especially by the most noble power of it, called the will.' [1]

St. Teresa [2] says : ' The soul now seeks not and possesses not any other will than that of doing our Lord's will, and so it prays to Him to let it be so; it gives to Him the keys of its own will—henceforth the soul will have nothing of its own—all it seeks is to do everything for His glory and according to His Will.'

St. Teresa's phrase ' for His glory ' sounds forensic. Absence of self-assertion or a recognition of

---

[1] Butler, *op. cit.*, p. 320. *cf.* ' The prayer of loving attention is a matter for the will, and if directions are received [*i.e.*, intuitively] for instant obedience.' Augustine Baker, *Sancta Sophia,* quoted by Dom Butler, *op. cit.*, p. 321.

[2] St Teresa, Life, p. 154.

his own helplessness together with faith in a higher will than his own may lead a man to give up the keys of his own will and to do everything according to the higher will, but the religious idea of God's glory can hardly enter into the process. The subject brings the faculty of will into conformity with the Divine Will, in order that he may do the Divine Will and not his own—he has no will of his own, just as a true soldier has none in respect of the command of his superior, though in carrying out the command he exercises all his faculties—and his pre-occupation with or absorption in the Divine Will leaves no room for the idea of God's glory, unless we define ' God's glory ' as ' the living man.' Even so, the man has no thought of his own life; he regards himself as the instrument of Another.

The Illuminative Way is followed, according to St. John of the Cross, by another Dark Night, the Dark Night of the Spirit, a period of aridity corresponding to the Dark Night of the Sense.

The book, called the *Dark Night of the Soul,* in which St. John discusses both these periods, is a piece of acute psychological analysis of something that is not unusual in the development of the spiritual life. The view that we are to accept these periods as inevitable stages is comforting to those who experience such depressions. They feel, and feel truly, that they need not strive; they have only to exercise patience in the certainty that they will emerge. Yet the recognition of the ' homeliness ' of God may preserve the contemplative not *through* but *from* the Dark Night.

Emerging from the Dark Night of the Spirit the soul enters upon the life of union.

IV

The philosophy [1] that justifies the adoption of the Scheme is implicit in the previous pages, but I will draw it out briefly.

(1) The first tenet is Eckhart's *intuitus mysticus* or Abbé Bremond's *primo*. ' There is another " thought " than abstract and discursive thought; another knowledge than conceptual and rational knowledge.' This faculty of intuition always corresponds to the intuition—the eye for the light corresponds to the light, the seeing is kindred to the thing seen—and when intuition concerns the supernatural it is called *intuitus mysticus*. There is a strange reluctance among writers on the traditional view of Mysticism to acknowledge that the intuition of a poet or of a poetic mind or of a mind in its poetic moments is the same faculty or gift as the intuition of a mystic. The pre-occupation of the mind determines the character of the intuition. For example, the mind of a physician may be intensely pre-occupied with medical treatment and his intuition will have that character. He is said to have a ' flair ' for diagnosis. In the same way the mystic's intuitions concern God, because his mind is pre-occupied with τὰ τοῦ θεοῦ and not with τὰ τῶν ἀνθρώπων (the things that be of men).

St. Augustine attempts to define more closely the nature and exercise of this faculty :

[1] I would refer the reader to *Studies in Early Mysticism in the Near and Middle East* by Margaret Smith (Sheldon Press, 1931).

' I entered and saw as it were with an eye of my soul above the same eye of my soul, above my mind an unchangeable light, not the light that is common and clear to all flesh nor as if it were a greater of the same kind but as if it shone altogether more brightly and occupied " all-thing " with its greatness.' [1]

There is no warrant in this philosophical tenet for teaching the ultimate disappearance of individuality in the Divine Substance. What change is brought about by death does not concern us, in respect of man's faculties as they are exercised here. Plotinus held that death only means that ' the actors change their masks ' (referring, of course, to the Greek custom of wearing one mask for comedy and another for tragedy), but he also taught that ' if any man seeks in the good life anything beyond the good life itself, it is not the good life which he is seeking.' Man, according to Plotinus, should exercise this faculty of his with a view to the good life or to the recognition of Beauty (τὸ καλόν)—which is the same thing. It is when you are ' self-gathered in the purity of your being ' that you have an eye for the ' mighty Beauty.'

This gift of intuition is the endowment of man. It is not confined to the few; it can and may be exercised by any man in any place.

(2) The second tenet is, that man has a share in the Divine Life. This is often called the doctrine of the Divine Spark.

' We must keep in mind that God dwells in a secret

[1] Transl. from *Confessions of St. Augustine* (Cambridge Patristic Texts, by Gibb & Montgomery, 1908) Liber vii, IX,

and hidden way in all souls, in their very substance, for if He did not, they could not exist at all.' [1]

Or, as Walter Hilton teaches, God Himself is the ground of the soul, which was made in his image and ' in the first shaping was wonderfully bright and fair, full of burning love and spiritual light.' [2]

A similar, if not the same tenet, seems to underlie Plotinus's description of Evil : ' Evil is not alone. By virtue of the nature of the Good, and of the power of Good, it is not Evil only. It appears, necessarily, bound around in bonds of Beauty like some captive bound in fetters of gold; and, beneath these, it is hidden, so that, while it must exist, it may not be seen by the gods, and that men need not always have evil before their eyes, but that when it comes before them they may still not be destitute of images of the Good and Beautiful for their remembrance.' [3]

And again : ' Wickedness is always human, *being mixed with something contrary to itself.*' [4]

The last words of Plotinus reported by Porphyry were : ' I have been a long time waiting for you; I am striving to give back the Divine in myself to the Divine in the All.'

With this may, perhaps, be correlated the doctrine of Eternity. Inge [5] sums up in these words : ' Eternity is on one side an ethical postulate. Without it

---

[1] *The Living Flame* by St John of the Cross, Stanza iv, 14. *cf. Mysticism: Its Nature and Value* by A. B. Sharpe, p. 143.

[2] *The Scale of Perfection* by Walter Hilton, 1, 3.

[3] *op. cit.,* S. MacKenna's Translation I, 8, 82.

[4] *cf.* Shakespeare's Henry V: ' There is a soul of goodness in things evil ' (which is really more accurate). I would draw the reader's attention to *Shakespearean Tragedy* by A. C. Bradley, especially Lecture viii, pp. 325ff.

[5] *The Philosophy of Plotinus* by W. R. Inge (Longmans, 1918), II, p. 101.

the whole life of will and purpose would be stultified. All purpose looks towards some end to be realised. But if time in its course hurls all its own products into nothingness—if there is no eternal background against which all happenings in life are defined, and by which they are judged, the notion of purpose is destroyed. The existence of human will and reason becomes incomprehensible.'

The tenet of the Divine Spark concerns not only the experiences of this life but the life of the world to come. For Plotinus, it is upon this tenet that the justification of the Scheme ultimately rests. He teaches the Scheme : purification, enlightenment, unification. There is no trace, however, in his teaching of the dereliction, called by St. John of the Cross, the Dark Night. Plotinus considers contemplation incomplete without creative activity. In his own words : ' We *are* the activity of Spirit.' But the highest stage is based upon the doctrine that ' there is progress even yonder.'

(3) The third tenet is : that none can attain to a direct knowledge of God except through the purification from self.

Once more, St. Augustine [1] : ' If to anyone the tumult of flesh were hushed, the appearances of earth and waters and air were hushed, hushed also the heavens and the very soul itself were hushed to itself and were to go beyond itself by not thinking on itself ; and dreams and revelations through images were hushed, and every tongue and every sign and whatever is of a transient character altogether hushed—

---

[1] Trans. from *op. cit.*, ix, 10.

since, if there were any to hear, all these say : " We have not made ourselves, but He has made us who abides for ever "—If, these things said, they are now silent, since they have pricked up the ear towards Him who has made them, and He Himself alone speaks, not through them, but through Himself, so that we may hear His word, not through the tongue of the flesh, nor through the voice of an angel, nor through the thunder nor through any similitude, but we hear Himself, whom we love in these things, Himself without these things, as if now we push ourselves out and with a swift thought touch the eternal wisdom abiding over all things ; if this were to go on and other visions of a far different character were withdrawn, and this one were to grip and absorb and plunge into interior joys the beholder, so that eternal life were like this moment of insight for which we have been sighing, is not this : " Enter into the joy of Thy Lord " ? And when shall this entrance be ? " When we all rise shall we be changed " ? '

(4) The fourth tenet is : that the controlling, unifying, and inspiring power of the soul in its ascent is Love.

There is no need for me to illustrate or support this tenet. In a sense, all that I have written up to this point proclaims it. Love is the air we breathe. Love is the ocean into which we adventure. Love presides over our life. Love reconciles, brings all things into one. Love is the fire that absorbs us, with more violence and completeness than a burning mountain absorbs a drop of water. And for a Christian the great placarding of

Love is not in the things that have pricked up the
ear to Him who made them but in a Man hanging
upon a Cross. That, too, is the eternal mirror of
Love, into which a man may look to know himself
for what he is and God for the End towards which he
moves.

I may refer to some English poems. *Quia amore
langueo*,[1] Francis Thompson's *Hound of Heaven*,
and Gerard Hopkins's *The Blessed Virgin compared
to the Air we Breathe* [2] illustrate the tenet just stated.

Browning's ' magnificent *Saul*,' as Bremond calls
it, tells of the spiritual progress of David from his
sense of the instinctive joys of animals and children
up to his intuition of Christ whose death in the Divine
Image was His great good deed for the world. Saul
is ' converted ' by his singing and David, as he goes
home, feels that Nature is transfigured. There is a
similar progress in John Masefield's *Everlasting
Mercy*, but painful at first, a kicking against the
pricks, of Saul Kane from his first dim sense of his
own unfairness and moral inferiority up to his
intuition of Christ knocking at the door. Here, also,
as he walks through the fields and lanes in the early
dawn, there is the feeling of the transfiguration of
Nature.

There is a spiritual progress in William Langland's
Vision of *Do Wel, Do Bet and Do Best*. Do Wel
is rectitude. Do Bet adds loving kindness and closes
in Christ's good deed and the harrowing of Hell.
Do Best is difficult to interpret. We are back again

[1] Oxford Book of English Mystical Verse, p. 6.   [2] *op. cit.*, p. 56.

in the awful conditions of the real world. Has Christ risen in vain, for here is Antichrist flourishing, bringing in his train Eld and Death through the great plague? At the end Conscience rises and goes forth to seek Piers Plowman. There is no Beatific Vision in this life. Hell has been harrowed, the duke of that place has been forced to unbar, but the victory is still to win for the enlightened conscience. Conscience is not an individual conscience but the conscience of Everyman. The individual is not satisfied to be saved alone [1]; he identifies himself with the soul of humanity.

In another aspect the renewed onslaught of Antichrist in the Vision of Do Best may be said to correspond to the Dark Night of the Spirit from which Conscience rises to seek Piers Plowman, that is to say, to reach the life of union.

IV

Asceticism is closely associated with praying. In fact, the Scheme of Prayer is often called the Ascetical Scheme. Self-denial and self-discipline are carried to the extreme of repression and self-torture. The most striking example in medieval times is the Blessed Henry Suso. I will quote a passage—by no means in full—from a book he wrote himself, *The Life of the Blessed Henry Suso*. It is written in the third person.[2]

[1] *cf.* Matthew Arnold's *Rugby Chapel.*

[2] *The Life of the Blessed Henry Suso,* by Himself, Trans. by T. F. Knox, 1865, 1913 (Methuen). Introd. by W. R. Inge. p. 46*ff.*

Suso was born at Ueberlingen A.D. 1300. At 13 he entered the Dominican convent at Constance, and after some years was sent to pursue his

' He was in his youth of a temperament full of fire
and life; and when this began to make itself felt, and
he perceived what a heavy burden he had in himself,
it was very bitter and grievous unto him and he
sought by many devices and great penances, how he
might bring his body into subjection to his spirit.
He wore for a long time a hair shirt and an iron
chain, until the blood ran from him; so that he was
obliged to leave them off. He secretly caused an
under-garment to be made for him; and in the under-
garment he had straps of leather fixed, into which a
hundred and fifty brass nails, pointed and filed sharp
were driven, and the points of the nails were always
turned towards the flesh.'

He devised other things of the like nature. He con-
tinued these tormenting exercises *for about sixteen
years* !

' . . . Above all his other exercises, he had a
longing desire to bear upon his body something which
might betoken a sensible sympathy with the painful
sufferings of his crucified Lord. To this end he made
for himself a wooden cross, in length about a man's
span, and of corresponding breadth, and he drove
into it thirty iron nails, intending to represent by
them all his Lord's wounds and love-tokens. He
placed this cross upon his bare back between his

---

studies at the University of Cologne. He refused the doctorate of theology
and from that time lived the life of an industrious confessor and preacher.
He died at Ulm on Jan. 25th, 1365. His mental sufferings through the
scandalising of a wicked woman were far harder to bear than his bodily
penances (pp. 154-170). His book has great attraction, in spite of these
stories of his sufferings, for he was a very lovable and humane man.
His doctrine derives from Eckhart, whose disciple he was. I may refer
the reader to the following pages of *The Life*: 19, 29, 60, 69, 103, 109,
114, 228, 232, 238, 240, 248.

shoulders on the flesh, and he bore it continually day and night in honour of his crucified Lord. Afterwards, in the last year, he drove into it besides seven needles . . .

' Once upon a time he had been so much off his guard as to take into his hands the hands of two maidens, who were sitting beside him in a public place though without any bad intention. He soon repented of this unguardedness and he considered that this inordinate pleasure must be atoned for by penance. As soon as he left the maidens, and had come into his chapel to his place of privacy, he struck himself upon the cross for this misdeed, so that the pointed nails stuck into his back. He moreover laid himself under an interdict for this fault, and would not allow himself after matins to go into the chapter-room, his usual place of prayer, to meet the heavenly spirits, who were wont to appear to him during his contemplation. At length, desiring to atone completely for this misdeed, he summoned courage and fell at the Judge's feet, and took a discipline in his presence upon the cross; and then going round and round on every side before the saints, he took thirty disciplines, till the blood ran down his back. In this way he atoned very bitterly for the inordinate pleasure which he had allowed himself.'

He did even more than this to atone, but I need not go on.

I have sometimes wondered what psychological connection there is between Henry Suso and similar self-torturers and the men of very various ages whom I visited for a while in a ward reserved for S.I.'s during the War. The men who inflicted wounds upon themselves were afraid to face what was coming to them. Their spirit was consternated, as I suppose Suso's spirit was by the fear that the fire and life of his temperament would get the mastery. The S.I.'s were nursed until they were well enough to stand their trial at a place everyone called ' Bo-sheep.' I know from my own experience what it is to desire pain in order to relieve mental suffering, and when I suffered *accidental* pain I was very glad.

It must be remembered that this form of asceticism was not confined to the Middle Ages. St. John of the Cross, who was contemporary with Shakespeare, seems in some passages of his treatise about Mysticism, the *Ascent of Mount Carmel,* to be the enemy of all natural delights and joys. The eye must be purged of all joy in seeing, the ear of all joy in hearing.

' It is also vanity for a wife or a husband to rejoice in marriage, for they know not whether they shall serve God better in that state . . . He that is married ought to live with freedom of heart, as if he had not been married.' [1]

And in at least one of the religious houses established in the Church of England as a result of the Oxford Movement, self-torture was tried as a means of bringing the body into subjection to the spirit. It was abandoned because of the realisation that in driving out one temptation you may let in a worse.

The word ' asceticism ' is, of course, a verb-substantive, and the Greek verb from which it derives

[1] *Ascent,* p. 289.

means ' to exercise.' The athlete knows the need of exercising. All sensible men acknowledge the need. But this generation is hyper-sensitive to bodily pain. So far from acknowledging the need of pain, it sees no use in it at all, except, perhaps, the use expressed in the proverbial saying : ' The burnt child dreads the fire.' Self-inflicted pain is a mark of madness or disease. We shudder at the excesses of men like Suso, and we also laugh at them as absurd.

Nor have we much sympathy with those who deny themselves the ordinary gratifications of life; we look for some abnormality or warping of character as the result of such repressions. And those who hold a sacramental view of marriage are outraged by the tendency of the rigid ascetic to regard the marriage-relationship as the chief of all sensual gratifications.

Beyond the self-discipline which every sensible person acknowledges to be imperative, there is no *necessary* connection between mysticism and asceticism, as commonly understood. Indeed, Richard de St. Victor [1] speaks of the inadequacy of a man's efforts in this direction. He is commenting on what seems to be at first sight an uninspiring verse of a psalm : ' Moses and Aaron among his priests and Samuel among such as call upon his name.' Under the heading of Aaron, the type of the priest who implores the help of God, he instances the man who has the will to make spiritual progress and practises self-denial and imposes upon himself hard tasks, and yet is disappointed and tries and fails. He does not

[1] Richard, a member of the Order of Victorines (Fr.), died in 1173. He was a pupil of the great Hugh (1096-1141). The reference is to *Adnotationes Mysticae in Psalmos* (Migne cxcvi), p. 329.

therefore abandon his efforts. He is not ' weaned at once from his self-confidence.' He perseveres in his running and making haste. Then after his renewed failure and consequent distress he enters the Holy of Holies—he has recourse to the ' altar within,' and as he makes his offering there, Aaron inaugurates his priestly office anew.

In 1916 I had occasion to visit the Trappist monastery on Mont des Cats—part of which was used as a hospital. Some of the monks were ' on leave ' and they had taken up immediately the severe manual labour, which is one of their austerities, and were maintaining their almost complete silence. I thought of Ecclesiasticus, who speaks of the work of the smith and the farmer as maintaining the fabric of the world, and of his assertion that their praying is in their working.

At any rate, I perceived that talking is not praying.

My own feeling about asceticism is that the appropriate discipline will be provided through the events of life. Suso made this discovery. His self-flagellations to atone for offences against God, for the inordinate pleasure of holding the hands of two maidens ' though without any bad intention,' and his efforts to subjugate the fire and life of his temperament, were a trivial discipline compared to the scandalising of a wicked woman, to which, by the way, he lent colour through his pity and love for the child of whom she accused him of being the father. His very simplicity and humaneness added an element to his suffering. And the chief trial of the patience of St. John of the Cross was not only his imprisonment in Toledo by the Calced Carmelites but the harsh treatment meted out to him, after his release from prison, by the Provincial of his own Order. If we wish to see and hear (in St. Augustine's sense) we must subject ourselves to events.

V

§ i

It will not be denied by any English student of Mysticism that the revival of interest in Mysticism began with the publication of Dean Inge's Bampton Lectures, *Christian Mysticism,* in 1899, and that the interest has been sustained and nourished by the books of Miss Evelyn Underhill. In 1901 appeared the version of *Revelations of Divine Love* by Julian of Norwich, transcribed from the Sloane MS. in the British Museum, modern spelling being adopted and words entirely obsolete rendered in modern English. The editor was Miss Grace Warrack. Dean Inge had referred to Lady Julian's account of her Shewings in his lectures, ' the beautiful but little known *Revelations.*' The ninth edition of Grace Warrack's transcription was issued in 1927. *The Cloud of Unknowing* was edited by Evelyn Underhill and published in 1912 and has since been reprinted. The best English text of *The Scale of Perfection* by Walter Hilton was edited by Evelyn Underhill in 1923. *The Life of Richard Rolle* together with an edition of his English Lyrics (now for the first time published) by Frances M. M. Comper followed in 1928 and was re-issued in a cheap edition in 1933. These writings of

English mystics all appeared in the fourteenth century: Richard Rolle (1290—1349), Lady Julian (1342—1413), the author of the *Cloud of Unknowing* (about 1350), and Walter Hilton (1330—1396). There are no other generally acknowledged English mystics, except perhaps Margery Kempe, until we come to Augustine Baker, whose *Sancta Sophia* was published in 1657.

Dean Inge has never concealed his opposition to the Roman Church, and Miss Underhill is a member of the Church of England. Yet their books have probably formed a first introduction of Mysticism to the great majority of Roman Catholics in England and America as well as to non-Romans. Indeed, Mysticism is often referred to as ' Dean Inge's thing,' and there is confusion of mind among his readers as to what the thing is.[1]

But Dean Inge, in his latest writing on the subject, *Introduction to Lyra Mystica* (1932), takes definitely

[1] This revival of interest in English-speaking countries coincides with a revival of interest in France. I have already mentioned De Maumigny's book. He and Poulain advocate a less stringent demand in the practice of mental prayer and are the advocates of ' acquired contemplation ' as distinguished from ' infused contemplation.' Saudreau (*L'État Mystique*) is of opinion that the prayer of passive union, which is the typical mystical experience, is within the reach of all devout men and women, and he is supported by Louis de Besse (*La Science de la prière*), by Lamballe (*La Contemplation*) and others. Both sides appeal to St Teresa de Jésus and St John of the Cross. Saudreau maintains that these Spanish Saints, when they speak of Contemplation, mean ' infused contemplation ' and teach that this Contemplation is open to all; but I gained the same impression as Poulain and De Maumigny, viz.: that their teaching is, that Contemplation is not open to all. These French theologians write *about* Mysticism as a way of praying.

My own opinion is, that *in any sense of practical use*, either for praying or for the hearing of poetry, Intuition is not a universal endowment of adult man (*cf.* Traherne, *Centuries of Meditation*, pp. 156, 157). And I think that this is recognised, though they do not express it in such a way, by the advocates of ' acquired contemplation.' De Maumigny says, in effect, that a devout person who treads the way of holiness need not be a mystic.

the traditional view: ' In very various degrees, all truly religious persons are mystics; *for the typical mystical experience is not trance or ecstasy; it is the act of prayer, when we are really praying, and feel that our prayers are being heard.*' [1]

In regard to the statement that all truly religious persons are mystics,' it is sufficient to remark that only the truly religious person can say whether he is a mystic or not, and if he is, he will probably keep silence, for not everyone is inclined to open up his secret thoughts or feels it ' laid upon him ' (in the Quaker phrase) to write a book about them. By ' in various degrees ' Dean Inge leaves room for the different stages, which he afterwards mentions, of the ascetical scheme. The word ' really ' may be interpreted ' intuitively.' Substitute ' know ' for ' feel ' and we include the typical mystical phenomenon, the intuition of God as present, or if we retain ' feel,' the intuitive contact with God. Use ' feel ' in Wordsworth's sense and we imply intuition.

Here is Dean Inge's description in the same writing [2] of the ascetical scheme. He applies it to mystics without distinction, including Plotinus, but he is thinking of St. John of the Cross. The experience of dereliction does not apply to Plotinus.

' Mystics not only admit, they insist on the inadequacy of their descriptions; and yet we can recognize the same chart of the land that is very far off, the same experience of purification, of enlightenment, of alternative rapture and dereliction [not ' alternative ' in the sense of swaying from one to the other], the

[1] Italics mine, p. xxix.   [2] p. xxxviii.

same recurrent images of blinding light and murky darkness, [this is not expressed as they would try to indicate it [1]] of growing detachment from all earthly interests, of simplification leading up to the ineffable experience of losing the separate self and becoming united with God Himself.'

He also speaks on another page of rare experiences of the mystics of the cloister, i.e., those who are engaged in contemplation, as being strictly not transferable.[2]

§ ii

The same writer refers to the Society of Friends as a purely mystical sect, ' which from that time (i.e., the time of George Fox) to this has taken the lead in almost every movement to apply Christian principles to practical problems.' But he adds, ' the Quakers have not contributed much to poetry.'

Sir Arthur Eddington refers [3] to the Quaker meetings for worship: ' We cannot argue that because natural mysticism is universally admitted in some degree therefore religious mysticism must necessarily be admitted; but objections to religious

[1] Plato in his VIIth Epistle draws a very necessary distinction between ' express ' and ' indicate.'

[2] William James (*Varieties of Religious Experience*, pp. 380-382) speaks of the four marks of the mystical mind: Ineffability, Noetic quality, Transiency, Passivity. These marks cannot be interpreted except by reference to Intuition. All intuitions are, strictly speaking, ineffable. By ' noetic quality ' William James must be seeking to indicate the quality that a truth intuitively apprehended has in comparison with the same truth (or, apparently, the same truth) arrived at by a process of reasoning: *e.g.* belief in immortality as an intuition or as an ethical postulate. Transiency also refers to intuition: the swiftness of the mode of apprehension (*quasi coruscatione perstringeris*) and therefore the transiency of the intuition itself. Passivity is, as we have seen, the condition of the receptive mind for intuition or vision.

[3] *Science and the Unseen World*, p. 47 (italics mine).

mysticism lose their force if they can equally be turned against natural mysticism. If we claim *that the experience which comes to us in our silent meetings is one of the precious moments that make up the fulness of life*, I do not see how science can gainsay us.' This is, still more emphatically, the view of mysticism as a way of praying.

' Elected Silence ' is the Friends' medium. ' Stillness of spirit ' is desired that the intuitive contact with God may succeed. They have passed beyond meditation and consideration (in the religious sense); they dispense with images and aids and make no acts of prayer; they are waiting in a bare room withdrawn into themselves, with nothing alien clinging to the authentic man. They believe that God's finger will touch them: He will establish relationship. They also respond in feeling after Him. They are seekers, and seeking implies discipline; their lives are more strictly disciplined than the lives of most men.

Of their relationship with God, Eddington speaks [1] with a joyousness that it is easy to understand : ' In the case of our human friends we take their existence for granted, not caring whether it is proven or not. Our relationship is such that we could read philosophical arguments designed to prove the non-existence of each other, and perhaps even be convinced by them—and then laugh together over so odd a conclusion. I think that is something of the same kind of security we should seek in our relationship with God. The most flawless proof of the existence of God is no substitute for it; and if we have that

[1] *op. cit.*, p. 70.

relationship the most convincing disproof is turned harmlessly aside. If I may say it with reverence, the soul and God laugh together over so odd a conclusion.'

This is simple and light-hearted as becomes a true mystic, who cannot describe one of those precious moments that make up the fulness of life and, moreover, does not wish to do so. That the Quakers have not contributed much to poetry is probably due to some deep-seated agreement with Abbé Bremond, that poetry being a way of *saying* blocks the path to the mystical experience. They have something better to do than to write poetry. And they have something better to do in another sense that Dean Inge has hinted at : what they gather in contemplation they give out in love. It is not only that they take the lead in applying Christian principles—whatever those may be—to practical problems, their contacts with their fellow-men retain something of that relationship with God of which you have heard Eddington speak.

§ iii

I will refer briefly to a religious movement within the Church of England. The Oxford Movement is usually dated as beginning on July 14th, 1833, with the Assize Sermon, delivered by John Keble. The text of his sermon was : ' Holiness, without which no man can see the Lord.' [1] By ' seeing the Lord ' I suppose he meant the intuition of God as present, in this life, and the enjoyment of the Beatific Vision,

[1] Heb, 12, 14.

after death. ' Holiness ' is the key-note of the move-ment. The ascetical teaching of their leaders was reflected in their own life of prayer : the way of holiness. There seemed to be, at first, a local and narrow application. But they broke down religious insularity and, as Mill said, ' opened, broadened, deepened the issues and meaning of European history.' W. G. Peck [1] shows that their social action, principally in the slums [2] and in humanizing the old Church-and-State views, was greater than their doctrinal effect. Once again they gave out in love what they gathered in contemplation. It began, however, in the traditional methodism of praying.

VI

§ i

In the pride and glory of the revelation of God in Christ Jesus, Christians find it difficult to appreciate a non-Christian's religion. But the religion of the ancient Greeks, if it is at all at the level of their other spiritual achievements, should be worth studying and appreciating. Recent researches of scholars—and I am thinking especially of Dr L. R. Farnell—have revealed the truth ' that the indebtedness of Christian

---

[1] *The Social Implications of the Oxford Movement* (1933), *passim.*

[2] I happened to be visiting a friend, who was at that time Rector of Kenton in Devonshire. The day was a Friday in Lent and, on the previous Wednesday, Father Wainwright, the Vicar of St Peter's, London Docks, had come to Kenton to preach. After his sermon, he said to my friend : ' I am afraid I was rather inaudible. The fact is, that just as I was coming away, a woman came to see me, and I hadn't any money except my fare down here, *so I gave her my teeth.*'

dogma and ritual to the later Hellenic paganism was
far greater than used to be supposed.' [1]

Wordsworth [2] speaks of pagans as ' suckled in a
creed outworn,' but they were not suckled in a creed
in our precise sense. Their religion was worship—
praying—and their askesis for praying was purifica-
tion. In the list of rules concerning fitting entrance
into a temple found inscribed at Rhodes in the time
of Hadrian, ' the first and greatest rule is to be pure
and unblemished in hand and heart and to be free
from an evil conscience.' [3]

I was lingering in Liverpool Cathedral one morn-
ing, when a stranger asked me to tell him about the
building. I asked him if he had seen the Chapel of
the Holy Spirit. He said, ' Indeed, yes. That
would invite even a pagan to pray.' He voiced a
truth about the chapel and a common opinion about
pagans : they are people who do not pray.

The result is, that when we go back to the original
μύστης and μυστικός and learn that the verb from
which these words derive is μύειν, to keep silence, we
are apt to pass over the original Greek use of ' mystic '
and ' mystical ' as having little or no connection with
the modern use. We easily acquiesce in the notion
that the Greek who was initiated into the mysteries
of worship kept silence about his mystical experience
because he was forbidden to speak : it was not lawful
for him to give utterance to what he knew. We do
not realise that his experience like that of St. Augus-
tine, of Eckhart, of St. John of the Cross and, to a

[1] Outline-History of Greek Religion by L. R. Farnell (1921), p. 157.
[2] ' The world is too much with us . . .'
[3] Corpus Inscriptionum Graecarum, Ins. Mar, Aeg., I, 789.

large extent, of the Lady Julian was ineffable and strictly speaking non-transferable.

The earliest record of the Eleusinian mysteries is to be found in the Homeric hymn to Demeter, which cannot be later than the close of the seventh century B.C.[1] They appear there as appealing to the whole Hellenic world, and their special promise to the initiated is the happiness of the soul after death. It would be a poor appreciation of God's witness of Himself that did not see in this, at least, an adumbration, of the Christian mystical experience, ' the intuition of God as present,' in this life, and the Beatific Vision after death. The initiation was open to women as well as men and occasionally to slaves. Many scholars have laboured to solve the problems concerning their ritual, their doctrine and their inner significance. ' Careful criticism shows that, though a simple form of sacrament was part of the preliminary service, the real pivot of the mystery was not this but a solemn pageant in which certain sacred things fraught with mystic power were shown to the eyes of the initiated, who also were allowed to witness mimetic performances showing the action and passion of a divine drama, the Abduction of the Daughter, the sorrow and long search of the Mother, the Holy Marriage of reconciliation, possibly the birth of a holy infant.'

One may well believe that those who saw these things in the Hall of Mysteries at Eleusis were not less affected by what they saw than those who attend a Passion Play. They were even more affected, for

[1] Farnell, *op. cit.*, p. 85.

the representation was not to them a play, but in a sense the unfolding of Realities, and one can imagine that the initiates carried away an abiding feeling of communion with the Power outside and greater than themselves.

' We must regard them,' says Dr Farnell, ' as the highest and most spiritual product of the pure Hellenic religion, investing it with an atmosphere of mystery and awe that was generally lacking in the public cult, and which was unperturbed at Eleusis by any violence of morbid ecstasy such as marked the Phrygian and some of the Orphic rites.'

The influence and power of appeal of these mysteries do not appear to have waned until the introduction of Christianity.

The Hellenic religion was anthropomorphic. Demeter began to be worshipped when it was almost forgotten that she was Mother-Earth. The uncouth type of a horse-headed Demeter was transformed into a beautiful human form by the coin-artist of Phigaleia. She wears a necklace with a horse-hoof as its pendant. Again, the winds (Anemoi) were scarcely fitted for civic life, but Boreas, having a personal name, was actually worshipped as Πολίτης. Aristophanes, drawing a distinction between the religions of the Greek and Barbarians says : ' They worship Sun and Moon, we worship real Gods such as Apollo and Hermes.' [1] The Greeks were not worshippers of Nature, as Wordsworth declared himself to be [2]; they worshipped personal Gods.

Their Art helped their worship, or was the expres-

[1] *Pax,* 410.   [2] *Tintern Abbey.*

sion of their worship. Who that has seen Leonardo da Vinci's cartoon of the Mother of our Lord with her mother can fail to understand the feeling of Æmilius Paulus, the alien Roman, when he looked on the Zeus Olympios of Pheidias and acknowledged the thrill of the ' real presence ' ? [1]

One may perhaps take the ' divine ' Plutarch as a typical μύστης. He was born, about A.D. 45 or 50, at Chæronea in Bœotia. He studied at Athens under the philosopher Ammonius. He visited Egypt. Later in life, some time before A.D. 90, he was at Rome ' on public business.' He continued there long enough to give lectures which attracted attention. He returned to Chæronea, which he was loth ' to make less by the withdrawal of even one inhabitant,' and spent the remainder of his life there. He was archon in the town and officiated for many years as a priest of Apollo, apparently at Delphi.[2]

Clough says [3] that ' his mind in his biographic memoirs is continually running on the Aristotelian Ethics and the high Platonic theories, which formed the religion of the educated population of his time.' This sentence of Clough exhibits the same muddle of philosophy and religion as we have noticed elsewhere. Plutarch's religion was not Platonic philosophy. His religion concerned worship and the things revealed in worship. His religion was not even essentially connected with his office as a priest of Apollo. His religion was mysticism. It was in praying that he experienced those precious moments that make up the

[1] Livy, 45, 28.
[2] Introduction to *Plutarch's Lives* by Arthur Hugh Clough (Dent), 1910.
[3] *op. cit.*, p. xviii.

fulness of life. His wife Timoxena was also a mystic.
They had both been initiated into the Dionysiac
mysteries. He was away from home when their one
daughter, born to them late in life, died. He wrote
to her [1]: 'Plutarch to his wife, greeting. The
messengers you sent to announce our child's death,
apparently missed the road to Athens. I was told
about my daughter on reaching Tanagra . . . What
our loss really amounts to, I know and estimate for
myself.' He dwells on the child's sweet temper and
pretty ways. But for consolation he closes with his
belief in the happiness of each human soul after
death, the belief being fortified by the tradition of
their ancestors and their own experiences in the mys-
tical worship of Dionysos.[2]

§ ii

Mystics were many in Greece when Dionysius (so-
named after Dionysos), a member of the Areopagus,
was converted to Christianity [3] by St. Paul. Various
works are attributed to him : *The Celestial Hierarchy,
The Ecclesiastical Hierarchy, Concerning the Names
of God, Mystical Theology, Epistles* and a *Liturgy*.
The book, *Mystical Theology*, usually known as *Theo-
logia Mystica*, because it was translated into Latin by
Duns Scotus Erigena [4] in the early Middle Ages, is

---

[1] *Consol. ad uxor,* quoted in *op. cit.,* p. x.

[2] Plutarch was not only a conscientious and devoted citizen and
punctilious and faithful priest and pious man, but he was cheerful and
amiable and humorous. He is the author of the famous question,
'Which existed first, the hen or the egg?' (The Symposiac, or After-
Dinner Questions).

[3] Acts xvii, 34.

[4] Duns Scotus is an important person in the development of Psychology.

of great importance in fixing the name and nature of Mysticism. Critics, after much discussion, are generally agreed that *Theologia Mystica,* as also the other works named, were written by a Christian Neoplatonist of the fourth century and the writer is referred to as pseudo-Dionysius.

I suggest that ' pseudo ' conveys a false impression and that the attribution of the works to Dionysius, the companion of St. Paul, preserves a true tradition and that the instruction given in those works was actually due to Dionysius. This instruction was intended for Greek converts or to persuade his fellow-countrymen and to lead them into the Christian fold. He was especially anxious to show the μύσται that their way of praying was consonant with Christianity and that Christ and not Demeter or Dionysos could satisfy their craving for an intimate apprehension of God in praying. His work was complementary to the Epistles of St. Paul.

The author [1] makes frequent reference to two writings that have been lost : *Symbolic Theology* and *Theological Institutions.*

We are making use of symbols when we speak of God as one who inhabits places or clothes himself with ornaments or as one who rages or grieves or sleeps or awakes. This refers not only, or even primarily, to the Old Testament Scriptures but to the current Greek notions. .

In *Theological Institutions* he treats of the Divine Unity, of the Trinity, of the Fatherhood and Sonship, of the Incarnation.

[1] I make use of *L'État Mystique* by Auguste Saudreau, especially pp. 21-27.

In *Concerning the Divine Names* he explains why God is called the good, life, wisdom, strength.

The cardinal sentence in *The Ecclesiastical Hierarchy* [1]—the hierarchy being organised by God to lead His people to their perfection—is : ' The common term of the whole hierarchy is charity towards God, the charity produced by the breath of God which unites the soul to Himself.'

Then he comes to the way by which one attains to the perfect knowledge [2]: the way of praying, when the soul is united to God in a union of love and receives a light which reveals God as an incomprehensible and ineffable Being. This is the true knowledge of God. Mystical Theology is this knowledge. It is in praying that man is raised to the sublime contemplation of the grandeurs of the Divine Goodness.

' The symbol persuades of and inculcates the truth in question; the mystical, the inexpressible, pushes towards God and unites with Him by a *kind of initiation* [3] which no master can teach.'

Saudreau quotes a passage from the Commentary on Dionysius by the Blessed Albert the Great : ' La science qui procède des données de la raison met dans tout leur jour les verités qu'elle déduit, mais cette science (mystique) ne procède pas des données de la raison, elle procède plutôt *d'une certaine lumière divine*, qui n'est pas l'affirmation (nette et précise) d'une verité. L'objet saisi par l'âme (c'est Dieu lui-même), agit si fortement sur l'intelligence, que l'âme

[1] *Eccles. Hier.* 1, 3.

[2] I quote from *The Divine Names* and the *Epistles* as well as *Theologia Mystica*.

[3] Italics mine.

veut à tout prix s'unir à Lui. Cet objet étant au-dessus de la portée de l'intelligence s'appuie sur quelque chose qui n'est pas determiné.'

St. John of the Cross speaks to the same effect in the *Ascent of Mount Carmel*,[1] interpreting Isaiah xl, 18, 19. He insists on the failure of the understanding, the failure of the will, and the failure of the imagination. Mystical theology, which is contemplation, is the way of wisdom. He quotes ' St. Dionysius ' as calling it ' a ray of darkness.'

All this reduces to a belief in intuition for the highest ends of praying.

As I have said, *Theologia Mystica* fixed the traditional application of ' mystical.' We are used to the name Theology as applying to books about the Holy Scriptures. Theology is doctrinal or moral. This ' Theology ' is used of a way of praying, and the highest way of praying is contemplation. Mystical Theology is contemplation.

§ iii

Erigena's translation, *Theologia Mystica*, is said ' to have run across England like deer.' I take this to mean that it was read in the religious houses and, perhaps, by the secular clergy. It exerted great influence in other countries. In England the Barons' Wars, followed by the Renaissance (flowering late) and the Reformation, led to the decay or discredit of mystical theology. Religion became dissociated from praying. The great intuitive minds found

[1] *op. cit.*, pp. 96 and 97.

refuge in poetry and not in contemplation. Meanwhile the spirit of nationalism strengthened; Englishmen became conscious of a new freedom and a new power; they learned to trust their own thoughts. The sixteenth century saw the rise of poetical dramatists. Whenever religion is a matter of controversy or, in Francis Bacon's phrase, its condition is 'not very prosperous,' we see the rise of poets. The emergence of Blake, followed by the Romantic Revival, is another example. The divine gift of Intuition is justified of all her children.

The traditional view of mysticism was almost wholly lost. In England it was only preserved by the members of one derided society, who were called in contempt, Quakers.

VI

THE MYSTICAL OUTLOOK

VI

THE MYSTICAL OUTLOOK

BESIDES the traditional view of Mysticism as a way of praying, there is another strand of meaning attaching to ' mystic,' ' mystical ' and ' mysticism.' Much of the confusion about the name and nature of Mysticism is due to the tangling up of the two strands of meaning. They cross and recross, because both are essentially associated with Intuition. Without a belief in another kind of ' thought ' than abstract and discursive thought and another kind of knowledge than conceptual and rational knowledge, one cannot be a mystic in the traditional sense, nor can one have what has come to be called the ' mystical outlook.' But mysticism considered as an outlook is not the same as traditional mysticism.

Mysticism, considered as an outlook, is a way of seeing the great things in the small things, and the typical mystical phenomenon is the intuitive knowledge of the Great Thing. Mysticism, in this sense, is not *any* way of seeing but *a* way, and the mystical experience is an intuition. There is, again, no question of rational knowledge. The word ' perception ' applies only in the stages that lead up to the mystical outlook, and it is when intuition enters that the outlook begins to be mystical.

There is something here that corresponds to the difference between meditation and contemplation, or between the ' acquired ' contemplation of Poulain and ' infused ' contemplation. The difference may seem unimportant, but it is doubtful if the nature of the mystical outlook can be understood without it.

Perhaps an example or two from phenomena, of which I wish to speak at greater length later on, will help to show the importance of the difference.

The mystical outlook may be taken as supplying (in Eddington's phrase) the ' poetry of existence.' If one notices the minute arrangements that seem to obtain in existence, the notice may be merely an interested or delighted perception, or it may involve an intuition—the arrangements of life suddenly and overwhelmingly suggesting the infinite. Whereas the ' minute particulars ' (a common enough experience) are always mystical.

Again, a metaphor or a simile may involve an intuition or it may be merely a perception.

Nor shall my sword *sleep* in my hand

seems to me to involve an intuition, but the ' Homeric simile ' is only mental picturing, acute visualization. That is to say, the word ' sleep ' in Blake's verse is a kind of poetic experience, while Matthew Arnold's picture of the wealthy woman watching the household drudge (*Sohrab and Rustum*) is *viste*.

I

This strand of meaning originates with St. Paul. If we turn to the central experience of St. Paul's life [1] we find that it convinced him of the Resurrection of the Dead. I wish to take notice of the record of this experience as revealing the quality of St. Paul's mind, because his use of words depends upon the quality of his mind.

St. Paul's experience was of a vision on the road to Damascus. It was a vision of a light, as Robert Browning's was,[2] and he heard his name called, as Robert Browning did. He had a spiritual understanding or intuitive apprehension of clear and emphatic words. The hearing of his name was a word to his condition : ' Saul, Saul, why persecutest thou Me ? ' He asked, ' Who art Thou, Lord ? ' And the answer was, ' I am Jesus Whom thou persecutest. It is hard for thee to kick against the pricks.' He asked again, ' Lord, what wilt Thou have me to do ? ' And the answer was, that he would be told what to do.

St. Paul had the kind of mind that could see a great thing in a small thing. He realised at once that his persecution of ' this way ' was a persecution of the Lord. He also understood without any explanation that the little compressed parable of the ploughman guiding and controlling his recalcitrant oxen was an indication, common-seeming though it was, of the conflict that had been going on in his mind since the death of Stephen.

He found Greek words that could be given a Christian twist, so that a word indicating a small thing could be used to indicate a great thing. Agape, for example, was enlarged to mean the Divine Charity

[1] Acts ix, 3ff.　　　[2] *Christmas Eve.*

—Love, in the great sense. Musterion and (by impli-
cation) mustes and mustikos were also taken over into
the Christian service. The union was no longer
between God and the individual only; it was between
Christ and His Church. There were no secret rites
and special cults. All the Lord's people were μύσται,
for all were initiated by Baptism. Christians were
not divided into groups, for Christ was not divided,
and the Church was His Body. The Corinthians
could not say : ' I am of Paul; and I of Cephas; and
I of Apollos; and [worst of all !] I am of Christ.' [1]

The great μυστήριον was the mystery of God's will,
and this had been made known unto us.[2] The mystery
of the fellowship [3] is now revealed : a Church, a Body
of Christ, as large as the world.

The word is taken out of its old association with
praying, for praying is only a part of religion, which
really concerns the whole of life.

And so he turns to the fundamental human relation-
ship : marriage. The relationship is an indication,
common-seeming though it be, of the union between
Christ and His Church. ' For this cause shall a man
leave his father and his mother, and shall be joined
unto his wife, and they two shall be one flesh.' This,
he says, is a great mystery, ' but I speak concerning
Christ and the Church [4] (τὸ μυστήριον τοῦτο μέγα
ἐστίν, ἐγὼ δὲ λέγω εἰς Χριστὸν καὶ εἰς τὴν ἐκκλησίαν).
Even if St. Paul does not refer to the ' mystery-
religions ' (and it is hard to see how he could be
understood otherwise by Greek converts who were not
Jews) the Church has used the word 'mystical ' for

[1] I Cor. i, 12.   [2] Eph. i, 9.   [3] Eph. iii, 9.   [4] Eph. v, 31, 32.

what he intended. Marriage is said to signify the mystical union that is betwixt Christ and His Church,[1] and the mystical union is also spoken of as a ' spiritual marriage.'

It is strange that the first Christian writer, writing in Greek to Greek converts, by detaching the idea of mystical initiation and mystical union from praying and devotional religion, should have opened the way for a use of ' mystical ' that is common to religious and (so-called) irreligious alike. Eddington says [2] that we cannot argue from the almost universal admission of natural mysticism to the necessary admission of religious mysticism. The fact is that religious mysticism came first and natural mysticism can be traced to St. Paul's use of language.

II

There is another apparent paradox. Many Christian writers about mysticism as a way of praying lay little stress on the redemption wrought in Christ Jesus. Of course, ' l'ordre de la Rédemption ' is in their minds; it is inevitably the ground of what they write, but they are so busy in explaining and illustrating and even arguing about the different stages of the life of prayer that one misses what one finds in the English medievalists, who are much less precise about praying—a deep and aweful consciousness of the great Epiphany of the Son of God and His death in the Divine Image.

[1] In the Marriage Service of the Church of England, three times, for Eph. v, 31, 32 is quoted in the Exhortation to the married persons.
[2] *Science and the Unseen World*, p. 47.

Whereas, as soon as we come to consider the mystical outlook, we seem to be met with the necessity of a redemption, of a recovery of something that has been lost. For this capacity for seeing a great thing in a small thing is a childish capacity. Traherne says [1] : ' All appeared new, and strange at first, inexpressibly rare and delightful and beautiful . . . I was a little stranger, which at my entrance into the world was saluted and surrounded with innumerable joys. My knowledge was Divine. *I knew by intuition those things which, since my Apostasy, I collected again by the highest reason* . . . I was entertained like an Angel with the works of God in their splendour and glory . . . Is it not strange, that an infant should be the heir of the whole world, and see those mysteries which the books of the world never unfold ? '

Or, again, ' The corn was orient and immortal wheat, which should never be reaped nor was ever sown. I thought it had stood from everlasting to everlasting . . . Boys and Girls tumbling in the street, and playing, were moving jewels. I knew not that they were born or should die; but all things abided eternally as they were in their proper places.'

We need not consider Traherne's account of his own childhood; we can consider a child's toy. A child's toy is not a picture, an image, such as the images in churches : the Judge, the Stations, the Angels, the Crucifix (which is not a symbol but a representation). These are to help grown-ups, the apostates. Anything will do for a child. Any mother will say, ' You need not buy her an expensive toy;

[1] *Centuries of Meditation,* pp. 156, 157 (Italics mine).

she likes an old rag doll just as well.' She can see the great thing in the small thing. She can attain to the Great Thing. She has an intuitive knowledge of it.

One day, when I had visited a dingy little house in a dark street and had seen a little girl of four with the dreadful disease of lupus, I mentioned my visit, without really apprehending the fact that Sylvia, my daughter of the same age, was in the room. I noticed her when she darted off. I said, ' Where are you going?' She said, ' That little girl,' and ran up-stairs. She reappeared with a great yellow-haired doll. I guessed, or dimly guessed, what she thought of this doll, because I had gone with her to buy it and I had heard her talking about its future and ' all that.' I asked her what she intended to do. Again she said, ' That little girl.' I did not wish her to see the little girl—lupus is a shocking thing to see. Nor did I wish her to give up the doll. But she insisted in a passionately vehement way that brooked no gain-saying. She and I walked together to the dark house. She hugged her doll without saying a word. I do not know what deeps of love and sacrifice she was sounding. We came into the presence of the little girl. I watched Sylvia. There was not a sign of repulsion on her face. With a queenly kind of grace and a smile that would make the angels hide their faces she handed over her doll to the stranger, and from that moment to the time of her death she did not mention the doll again. Here is the Divine Charity in a child's toy.

After childhood and youth there does seem to be,

as Traherne says, a kind of increasing apostasy. The appropriate mode of apprehension is atrophied.

' Up to the age of thirty, or beyond it, poetry of many kinds, such as the works of Milton, Gray, Byron, Wordsworth, Coleridge, and Shelley gave me great pleasure, and even as a schoolboy I took intense delight in Shakespeare, especially in the historical plays. I have also said that pictures gave me considerable, and music very great delight. And now for many years I cannot endure to read a line of poetry; I have tried lately to read Shakespeare, and found it so intolerably dull that it nauseated me. I have also almost lost my taste for pictures and music.' [1]

A rag-doll to a child is a living symbol, the centre of her loveliest intuitions, and afterwards we may trace the gradual decline of symbols to ornaments or mere tokens or things without any poetic or religious significance. The pelican pecking at her breast and feeding her own young with her life-blood would hardly be understood now of Christ and His Church. The peacock spreading his tail would remind us of the garden of Warwick Castle—a beautiful thing enough—rather than of the Resurrection. ' I saw three ships come sailing by ' is preserved in an old carol. At one time everyone knew that the ship on the sea was the Church on the ocean of God's love.

The ring is now a token of marriage. It has a

[1] Autobiography of Charles Darwin (Thinkers Library), p. 73. *cf.* Wordsworth's *Ode on the Intimations of Immortality:*

> What though the radiance that was once so bright
> Be now for ever taken from my sight,
>   Though nothing can bring back the hour
> Of splendour in the grass, of glory in the flower . . .

noble history as a symbol. Plato in his *Phaedo*
attempts to prove the immortality of the soul through
the idea of a circle combined with his doctrine of
Anamnesis.[1] Plotinus employs the symbol for the
divinity within ourselves.[2] The Blessed Henry Suso
also employs the symbol : ' God is a circular ring,
whose centre is everywhere and circumference no-
where.' [3] Henry Vaughan [4] sees Eternity as a Ring :

> I saw Eternity the other night,
> Like a great ring of pure and endless light,
>   All calm, as it was bright;
> And round beneath it, Time in hours, days, years,
>   Driv'n by the spheres
> Like a vast shadow mov'd; in which the world
>   And all her train were hurled.

Robert Bridges uses the symbol in the *Testament
of Beauty* :

> and with inspiration of their [5] ampler air we see
> our Ethick split up shear and sharply atwain; two
>   kinds
> diverse in kind there be; the one of social need,
> lower, still holding backward to the clutch of earth,
> from old animal bondage unredeem'd; the other,
> higher and spiritual, that by personal affiance
> with beauty hath made escape, soaring away to where
> The Ring of Being closeth in the Vision of God.

Numbers were once regarded as speaking of God :
three, of His nature; seven, of His perfection; ten,
of His completeness. Or, the truths of God and of
His revelation were kept in mind by numbers. Cecil
Sharp gathered the Dilly Song [6] from Mrs Jane

---

[1] For the belief in pre-existence and the adherents thereto see *Pre-
existence and Reincarnation* by Wincenty Lutoslawski (Allen & Unwin),
1928.

[2] *Ennead* vi, 9, 8.   [3] *op. cit.*, p. 232.

[4] *Silex Scintillans* : Part II (1655), *The World.*

[5] *i.e.* the prophets of God IV [240].

[6] *Folk Songs from Somerset.* Fourth Series, p. 25. Cecil Sharp says
that Sullivan introduced a version of it in the *Yeomen of the Guard.*

Chapman of Harptree. The Dilly Song is cumulative. This sacred version of it has now become almost impossible to interpret. The last stanza reversed gives the sequence:

> One and one is all alone, and evermore shall be so [God Almighty]
>
> And two and two are the lily-white babes a-clothed all in green, O! [perhaps, the angels at Christ's birth]
>
> Three of them are thrivers (or, wisers) [The Three Wise Men—they throve in their search]
>
> And four are the gospel makers [The four Evangelists]
>
> Five are the flamboys under the boat [possibly the Feeding of the Five Thousand, told by all four Evangelists]
>
> And six are the six broad waiters [The six waterpots at Cana of Galilee: 'the first sign that Jesus did']
>
> Seven are the seven stars in the sky [The most excellent canopy]
>
> And eight are the eight commanders or 'Gabriel Angels' [God's messengers]
>
> Nine are the nine which brightly shine, or, 'the nine delights' [i.e. of Mary]
>
> And ten are the ten commandments [The moral code as interpreted by Christ]
>
> Eleven and eleven are the keys of heaven, or, 'Eleven and eleven is gone to heaven' ['The Twelve'—without Judas]
>
> Twelve are the twelve apostles [The Church remains].

III

I have spoken of the detachment from praying, leading on to the detachment from revealed religion. But the detachment was gradual. St. Paul applied his symbolic mind, filled with the all-sufficiency of Christ, to the history of religious development in the Old Testament Scriptures. The history, as indeed all history, was a shadow of Christ. He alone was the substance. In Him the shadows became substance in their own place, though they still remained shadows in another place. But the substance was a true substance and the shadow a true shadow. The modern complaint would be, that St. Paul's emphasis on these Old Testament ' substances ' as ' shadows ' of Christ was so strong that he seems to deprive them of any reality in themselves, as if they happened, not in a natural course of things, but in order to fore-shadow Christ.

The story of Hagar, the casting-out of the bond-woman and her son, is transformed into an allegory (ἅτινά ἐστιν ἀλληγορούμενα) of the two covenants: the one from Mount Sinai which answereth to Jerus-alem, which now is and is in bondage with her children . . . He does not say explicitly what the other covenant is, but we assume that it is the covenant of Jerusalem which is above. And his conclusion is: ' So then, brethren, we are not children of the bond-woman but of the free.' He takes us forward to Mount Sinai and from Sinai to the Jerusalem which now is, and his leaping mind does not pause to tell us that Sarah answers to the heavenly Jerusalem, and after interjecting a reference to Isaiah liv, 1, of which it is difficult to see the relevance, as neither Hagar nor Sarah was barren, he brings us back abruptly to the bondwoman.

This mode of interpretation, which is a seeing of a great thing in a small thing, led on to *Adnotationes Mysticae,* of which I have already given an example. The most famous of these mystical commentaries or mystical interpretations of Scripture is St. Bernard's *In Cantica Canticorum.*[1] The Song of Songs is now usually regarded as a love-song, but St. Bernard

[1] Bernard, b. 1090, d. 1153.

interprets it as of Christ and His Church, and the interpretation is accepted in the chapter-headings of the Authorised Version of the Bible. In his 23rd sermon Bernard speaks briefly of the ' threefold manner ' of interpreting Scripture [1] and Hugh de St. Victor, who corresponded with Bernard, teaches the method of interpretation in *De Sacramentis*.[2] Hugh's

[1] Migne clxxxiii Ed. 1854.

[2] lib. 1, prologue (Migne clxxvi, p. 184).

' The works of the restoration of man are the subject-matter of all holy scriptures . . . But though the works of restoration are the principal material of divine scripture, that it may proceed more competently to deal with them, it narrates, with a brevity that accords with faith, in the first chapter, the opening events and constitution of the works of creation . . . Then it records how man was made and constituted in the way of righteousness and discipline; afterwards it tells of man's fall, and lastly how he was restored. First then it portrays the material as it was made and founded; then the misery in guilt and punishment; then the reconstruction and mercy (*misericordia*) in the recognition of the truth and in the love of virtue; and lastly the native land (*patriam*) and joy of beatitude.

' Of this material divine scripture deals after a three-fold manner : in history, in allegory, and in tropology. History is the narrative of events, which is found in the prime meaning of the letter; allegory is when by that which is stated as a fact some other fact, past, present or future is signified; tropology is when by that which is stated as a fact something to be yet accomplished is signified . . .'

This threefold explanation was formulated by Origen, introduced to Western thought by St Augustine and taken up with special enthusiasm by St Bernard and the Victorines. The reason for their enthusiasm lies in the shrinking away from the ' natural ' meaning of many passages in the Old Testament as having to do with the will and character of God; and, while we are at liberty to acknowledge an admixture of error in the presentation of that will and character in the history of Israel, they were not permitted to do so, but were bound to a theory of literal or verbal inspiration, and they escaped from the burden of this theory in the manner briefly described in the above paragraph.

St Bernard appears to some to be more of a moralist than a mystic (in the traditional sense), but in his discussion of the text, ' The King hath brought me into his storerooms (*cellaria*) ' (Sermon xxiii, *In Cantica Canticorum*), he gives an account of his own ' mystical experience,' which has the authentic note. The Rev. Bertram Lester, S.S.M., to whom I am indebted for the translation of St Bernard and Hugh of St Victor, makes an interesting comparison between Bernard and Blake. He says that both men had their ' moments of mystical experience of reality,' and ' neither possessed sufficient self-criticism to distinguish these from mental pictures which have another source than reality.' But, while Bernard was diffident and welcomed outside criticism of his experience, Blake was not diffident at all.

pupil, Richard, was the likeliest for intuitions, and he was able to ' correct ' his intuitions by means of the tradition he had received.

The author of St. John's Gospel has a subtler method, if it can be called a method. I made a stumbling attempt to declare the nature of the gift in the *Seven Signs*. In the first three signs (' Water into Wine,' ' The Healing of the Nobleman's Son,' ' The Pool of Bethesda) I seemed to see Christ revealed as Creator, Redeemer and Sanctifier; and in the four following signs, the outward and visible acts that proclaimed the great truths of God's dealings with his people : e.g., I am in the midst of you, or, *tout court,* I am—the words ἐγώ εἰμι containing an implicit claim to be one with the Father; I am the Bread of Life; I am the Light of the World; I am the Resurrection and the Life. This, at first sight, may seem to be artificial, as if the acts were performed *ad hoc,* but when one looks at the acts from another side, one finds that they were all the outcome of a fellow-feeling with or compassion for those with whom Jesus was brought into contact. For example, the healing of the man blind from his birth was due to our Lord's compassion for him. The act also declared the truth of Christ the Light of the World and the whole life-experience of the blind man from his birth to the moment of his healing and after his healing as a revelation of God's glory.

It was after my attempt to shew all this that Arthur Clarke fell into the monologue mentioned in the first chapter of this book. His mind was full of parallels and analogies, and he seemed to accept without question the unity of Revelation. But the habit of mind or ' thought ' most impressive to me was not this quasi-symbolic habit nor even the recognition of unity, but something that went with it, and yet beyond it. He seemed to reach his conclusions at once and then to ratify them afterwards. I had the feeling that his recognition of unity, due, as he said, to the fact that all the New Testament writers were writing about one and the self-same Jesus, led him to leave himself open to the movement of the self-same Spirit. His simplifications were extraordinary, and after stating them he would proceed to show—in a half-apologetic manner—that they were reasonable. It seems to me now, that if one had set down, at the moment, the words that flowed from him in such an easy and unchecked stream, one might have had a collection of *adnotationes mysticae* superior to any-thing produced by St. Bernard or the Victorines.

I now perceive why he repeated what the Pope says at the end of his long day spent upon the Roman murder-case. Clarke's emphasis was on

> So may the truth be flashed out at one blow,
> And Guido see, one instant, and be saved.[1]

The intuition of truth may come to the worst of men. Indeed, the worst of men needs the intuition most. Clarke had probably known, during years of incessant ministry, many men with the same need as Guido, and recognised the religious and ethical value of intuitions at least as clearly as Browning.

---

[1] *The Ring and the Book*, x, 2127-8.

IV

We come to the men of intuition, to the poets them-selves, with this important consideration that both the poetic way of saying and the poetic experience really belong to humanity as a whole, so that while we draw illustrations from those who are called poets, the knowledge and experience of the poetry of exis-tence is shared by countless thousands who never write a line of poetry and have no acquaintance with the technique of prosody. In fact, the poetry of exis-tence may be experienced even in connection with occupations which seem entirely alien from it. Some human beings are as capable of making an approach to the poetry of existence out of a machine as others are out of Nature.

§ i

The poets may be almost known by their use of metaphor and simile and symbol.

They put them to many uses, and all readers of poetry will be familiar with these uses. In the main, they are to exalt a small thing into a great thing, or to show how great the common-seeming thing is, or to give poignancy to something that might otherwise pass unnoticed. But occasionally the process is reversed, and metaphor and simile are used to degrade the great thing.

Macbeth, who has the poet's make, exalts sleep [1] in lines already quoted, beginning

> Sleep that knits up the ravell'd sleave of care . . .

But at the end, when the milk of human kindness has all curdled in him, he uses the symbols of degradation :

> To-morrow and to-morrow, and to-morrow,
> Creeps in this petty pace from day to day,
> To the last syllable of recorded time;
> And all our yesterdays have lighted fools
> The way to dusty death. Out, out, brief candle!
> Life's but a walking shadow, a poor player
> That struts and frets his hour upon the stage,
> And then is heard no more; it is a tale
> Told by an idiot, full of sound and fury,
> Signifying nothing. [2]

One may compare with this Hamlet's language in his talk with Rosencrantz and Guildenstern : ' O God! I could be bounded in a nutshell and count myself king of infinite space.' But his ' bad dreams ' have reduced the great to less than little : ' this good frame, the earth, seems to me a sterile promontory : this most excellent canopy, the air, look you, this brave o'erhanging firmament, this majestical roof fretted with golden fire, why, it appears no other thing to me but a foul and pestilent congregation of

---

[1] Lady Macbeth speaks prosaically of sleep, ' You lack the season of all natures, sleep,' as who should say, ' Everyone needs sleep.' One of Macbeth's praises of sleep is ' the death of each day's life,' and, perhaps, in this light must be understood :

> . . . We are such stuff
> As dreams are made on, and our little life
> Is rounded with a sleep.

This, together with Horatio's : ' And flights of angels sing thee to thy rest,' may give us some inkling of Shakespeare's own view of death.

[2] *Macbeth*, Act v, Sc. v, 19*ff*.

vapours.   What a piece of work is man ! . . . And, yet, to me, what is this quintessence of dust ? ' [1]

The Homeric simile is a whole elaborated picture. Matthew Arnold uses it several times in *Sohrab and Rustum* (Sohrab is Rustum's son, whom the father has never seen) :—

> As some rich woman, on a winter's morn,
> Eyes through her silken curtains the poor drudge
> Who with numb blacken'd fingers makes her fire—
> At cock-crow, on a starlit winter's morn,
> When the frost flowers the whiten'd window-panes—
> And wonders how she lives, and what the thoughts
> Of that poor drudge may be; so Rustum eyed
> The unknown adventurous youth, who from afar
> Came seeking Rustum, and defying forth
> All the most valiant chiefs; long he perused
> His spirited air, and wonder'd who he was.
> For very young he seemed, tenderly rear'd;
> Like some young cypress, tall, and dark, and straight,
> Which in a queen's secluded garden throws
> Its slight dark shadow on the moonlit turf,
> By midnight to a bubbling fountain's sound—
> So slender Sohrab seem'd, so softy rear'd.
> And a deep pity entered Rustum's soul
> As he beheld him coming . . .

Walter de la Mare has unexpected turns.   For example, in his poem, *Hospital,* he speaks of the ' Ancient Tapster of this Hostel,' ' silent of foot, hooded and hollow of visage,' who pauses to peer out at someone lying there—a dreadful picture of Death —and continues :

> To him at length even we all keys must resign;
> And if he beckon, Stranger, thou too must follow—
> Love and all peace be thine.

§ ii

The chief associations of the ' poetic experience are with Nature or Children or with the experience of

[1] *Hamlet*, Act ii, Sc. ii.

Friendship or Marriage. Its result or content is an apprehension of unity or beauty or love or a sense of reconciliation or even of identification. In the small thing, meaning the temporary, transient thing, is seen the great thing, meaning the eternal and fadeless thing.

(a)

Concerning Nature, it was one of George Meredith's strongest convictions that the ' spirit of Nature at her loneliest and most " poetic " must be united to the spirit of everyday humanity at its commonest, until we can feel that the same essence stirs both.' [1]

Wordsworth's *Prelude*,[2] begun in his Quantock days (1798) and finished in 1804 and continually revised, was not published until after his death in 1850. It is an account of his increase in poetic knowledge, beginning with his early intuitions through Nature, showing how those intuitions progressed until his consecration for work as a poet [iv 330—346], and then tracing the gradual growth of his intuitions about Man. The turning point came with his meeting a discharged soldier [iv 400ff.] but Human Nature was not a ' punctual presence ' until much later. In London, however, he records his conviction that the ' Swarm of its inhabitants ' is not wholly an unmanageable sight

> . . . to him who looks
> In steadiness, who hath among least things
> An undersense of greatest; sees the parts
> As parts, but with a feeling of the whole [vii 709-712]

[1] *The Poetical Works of George Meredith*, with some Notes by G. M. Trevelyan, p. 581.

[2] I quote from the 1804 version in *Wordsworth's Prelude*, ed. by Ernest de Selincourt (1926).

Yet even in London,

> The Spirit of Nature was upon me here;
> The Soul of Beauty and enduring life
> Was present as a habit, and diffused,
> Through meagre lines and colours, and the press
> Of self-destroying, transitory things
> Composure and ennobling harmony [vii 735-740]

At length Man rose to a loftier height ' as of all visible creatures crown ' [viii 631].

Sometimes, Wordsworth's experience is hardly explicable except by reference to the mode of apprehension, which has been considered under ' Vision.' In Nature he saw something that was not seen by others, even though the actual forms and hues were there to be seen by anyone, and these forms and hues persisted ' as in a mirror ' and were allied to his affections. His intuitions about Man are not so brilliant, but they have a greater steadiness [1] and a more common-sense quality. He sees the parts as parts. He sees the indications of the small as well as of the great.

His feeling of unity came first through Nature. A poignant moment of contact with human nature ' at its commonest ' gave to this feeling a new element. The contact was with an artificer, who had stolen a short time from his work, and was sitting on the corner-stone of a low wall in an open square. The man had a sickly babe upon his knee. He had brought the child there for sunshine and to breathe the purer air. He took no note of any passer-by.

[1] See *Tintern Abbey* for the *unsteadiness* of the intuitions through Nature. At the end of that poem he seems to give up all certainty that they will recur, much less remain, and he falls back upon the idea that he will be of service to his sister.

He held the Child, and, bending over it,
As if he were afraid both of the sun
And of the air, which he had come to seek,
He eyed it with unutterable love [vii 855-8]

(b)

George William Russell (A.E.) and Edmund
Blunden have written almost as movingly about chil-
dren as Blake in his *Songs of Innocence* or Words-
worth in *We are Seven* or *To H. C.* or Francis
Thompson in his *Sister Songs*. A line from A.E.[1]
is often singing in my head:

On the laugh of a child I am borne to the joy of the
King.

And I have compelled my memory to hold this
from *Halfway House*:

Over the green the hour is tolling sweet,
The hammers chime in the forge, the children run
From school with shrill delight down sleepy street,
There where the last wall's pear-tree takes the sun
See the red bonnets and quaint caps come on.
Surely the wide lea trembles as they pass,
And it is earth-born joy that's whispering through
the rushy grass.[2]

John Masefield [3] is very near Blake:

And he who gives a child a treat
Makes joy-bells ring in Heaven's street,
And he who gives a child a home
Builds palaces in Kingdom come.

(c)

St. Augustine [4] has a pleasant picture of a friendly
circle in Carthage. He speaks of things that ' take ' [5]

[1] *Oxford Book of English Mystical Verse*, p. 500.
[2] p. 24.   [3] *Everlasting Mercy*.
[4] *Conf.*, iv, 13. *cf. Symposium of Plato*, 193D (Loeb Edition).
[5] *cf.* ' That did so take Eliza and our James ' (Ben Jonson on Shake-speare).

the mind, of laughing and talking and reading together, of dissenting from one another sometimes, without hatred, as if a man dissented from himself, and then of many agreements, teaching one another and learning from one another, longing for the absent ones with grief and welcoming the new-comers with joy. Then his language becomes more glowing and he speaks of the fellowship of lovers who show their love through their speech, through their looks and a thousand most pleasing gestures and set their minds on fire and ' out of many make one thing ' (*ex pluribus unum facere*).

This experience of unity through human relationships prepared him for the larger unity.

Traherne speaks of another intuition through friendship; the discernment of a strange power in ourselves of giving our Creator pleasure. ' We receive power to see ourselves amiable in another's soul and to delight and please another person. For it is impossible to delight a luke-warm person, or an alienated affection with giving crowns and sceptres, so as we may a person that violently loves us with our very presence and affections. By this we may discern what strange power God hath given to us by loving us infinitely. He giveth us a power more to please Him, than if we were able to create worlds and present them unto Him.' [1]

---

[1] *Centuries of Meditation*, pp. 121, 122. Compare with this a poem of his (*Oxford Book of English Mystical Verse*, p. 75) in which he speaks of *our* making God's works more glorious than He made them first. The poems of Thomas Traherne (1904) and his *Centuries of Meditation* (1908) were first printed from the Author's MS. and edited and published by Bertram Dobell, to whom we are much indebted. Traherne himself died in 1674 at the age of 38 or 39. At first, his *Centuries of Meditation* was meant for one person only.

(d)

Coventry Patmore held that ' woman's love to man is the model, the mode of the soul's love to God.' [1]

To Robert Browning marriage meant entrance into a new world, and he uses words that might befit the highest experience of a contemplative. Even the strange phrase of Dionysius, ' a ray of darkness,' is suggested. He can stand out of his own self on the world's side—the world's side is always exile—and praise as they praise, pretending even that their knowledge is real knowledge,

> But the best is when I glide from out them,
> Cross a step or two of dubious twilight,
> Come out on the other side, the novel
> Silent silver lights and darks undreamed of,
> Where I hush and bless myself with silence.[2]

And, after her death, he speaks not only of his wife as having been the gift by which he was best taught song, but of her even then as the minister of a spiritual imperative. He cannot begin his song without beseeching an interchange of grace, a splendour that was once her very thought, a benediction that was once her smile, so that what was again may be, despite the distance and the dark. Nor can he conclude without appealing to her ' realms of help ' for blessing, whether to glorify what he has done well or to tread out the marks of his stumbling.

> —Never conclude, but raising hand and head
> Thither where eyes, that cannot reach, yet yearn
> For all hope, all sustainment, all reward,
> Their utmost up and on,—so blessing back

[1] *Patmore* by Frederick Page, p. 144.   [2] *One Word More.*

In those thy realms of help, that heaven thy home,
Some whiteness which, I judge, thy face makes proud,
Some wanness where, I think, thy foot may fall.[1]

(e)

There is another flight of the ' Intuitive Soul,'
which I think of sometimes as reconciliation and
sometimes as identification. The indications of it
remind me of the strangely beautiful experience of
seeing *Britannia* sail when she was racing with
Valkyrie and of the instant association of this with
my walk in the woods. And the result was akin to
the conclusion of Shelley's *Ode to the West Wind*.
Shelley speaks of himself as the companion of the
Wind in his wanderings over heaven and prays the
Wind to lift him ' as a wave, a leaf, a cloud ' and
finally to be through his lips ' to unawakened earth
the trumpet of a prophecy.'

O Wind,
If Winter comes, can Spring be far behind?

We have seen Gerard Hopkins's identification of
himself with the skylark for the spiritual imperative
of Go on and Stop, but he also seems to experience
in himself the counterpart of what the skylark sees
and feels. The skylark's instinctive joys become the
poet's intuitive joys.

Through the velvety wind V-winged
To the nest's nook I balance and buoy
With a sweet joy of a sweet joy,
Sweet, of a sweet, of a sweet joy
Of a sweet—a sweet—sweet-joy.[2]

In John Masefield's *Good Friday* the Madman

[1] *The Ring and the Book* I, 1410ff.   [2] *op. cit.*, p. 84.

seems to identify himself with Jesus. ' God celebrates
the madman's funeral,' he says of the earthquake.
And in the darkness

> I have been scourged, blinded and crucified,
> My blood burns on the stones of every street
> In every town; wherever people meet
> I have been hounded down, in anguish died.
> .   .   .   .
> Those golden ones will loose the torted hands,[1]
> Smooth the scarred brow, gather the breaking soul
> Whose earthly moments drop like falling sands
> To leave the spirit whole.

The Madman has the secret of Wisdom and Beauty
because he can so sympathize with Christ's sufferings
as to feel them as his own. It is no demented identi-
fication. There have been madmen who saw them-
selves as Christ, in power, in uniqueness. This
Madman's identification of himself with Christ is one
that keeps the distinction clear. Jesus is their King
—Jesus is apart. Jesus is the righteous one who has
been very kind to him. And when the sentry asks,
' Was He a Jew ? ' the Madman answers, ' No.' He
himself is a Jew who has advanced beyond the cus-
toms of Jewry and has been made wise by being
blinded. Jesus *is* Wisdom and Beauty, of no particu-
lar race, but arising out of humanity and being Son
of Man. The Madman's ' No ' is an inspired word.
At the end of the play the Madman addresses the
unseen Jesus as ' Friend ' :

> Friend, it is over now,
> The passion, the sweat, the pains,
> Only the truth remains.

[1] *cf.* Richard Rolle (see page 67).

V

Perhaps it is a part of the poetry of existence to be conscious of Minute Arrangements. They are variously attributed to Providence or to a Divinity or to Fortune or to Chance. The religious person might say that our Father treats us as His children and sometimes lets us see His delicate, adjusting care of our lives in detail. The arrangement has to do with our lives now, and though it may be connected in the mind of a religious person with the life of the world to come, it has no essential connection with a belief in immortality or in the resurrection of the dead.

These arrangements, involving several people, it may be, are all common-seeming and, in a sense, natural : one man sends a telephone message instead of writing; another is a friend of someone else; a third happens to be in a certain place at a certain time—' It is all luck, d'ye see '—and these various happenings fit in with one another, and the issue of them is momentous for an individual. It is like the plot of a novel, except that the novelist, by exposing the arrangement, would lay himself open to the charge of making his fiction stranger than truth.

But it is not the plot of a novel. Considered dispassionately, it has the appearance of control by a Power outside. We are familiar with this control in ' Big Business ' and in War, exercised by some person who can pull all the strings or has his hand on the whole machine. He not only controls but corrects the mistakes of those under him or so manages that the purpose or end for which he is working is not baffled nor the machine thrown disastrously out of gear. The Power that seems to be at work in these Minute Arrangements has, it would appear, his own plan for each individual and these plans fit in with one another, dovetail so perfectly, that each seems to be the sole object of interest or care. The idea of such a possibility is bewildering to a finite intelligence. Yet sometimes we have an intuitive conviction that it is so—that what we have noticed for ourselves is true for all. It would seem that having noticed the arrangement once or twice, we need not take the trouble to notice it any more. We can feel the assurance that Horatio feels. Hamlet says, having noticed these minute arrangements, ' There's a divinity that shapes our ends, rough hew them how we may.' Horatio replies, ' 'Tis most certain.' Horatio may not have noticed these minute arrangements, but he is quite sure of Divine control : he does not need to notice.

Yet it is worth while noticing. A new law arises out of it—the law of ' Wait and see,' in the joyous expectation of what comes next. That is the Fool's way of living. But he is not like to horse and mule that have no understanding. He exercises his reason ; he makes use of his rational knowledge. Nor is he like the waggoner who called on Hercules when his cart fell into a rut. He puts his shoulder to the wheel and pushes with all his force.

May I be allowed to relate another experience of my own ? Fifteen years ago, as I write, I was waiting for a tram inside a barrier at the back of a great railway-station in an English Midland town. I had some time to wait, and several trams stopped in front of the barrier, before the one came that I wished to take. I saw many men and women enter trams, very diverse men and women, and the conviction came to me that every one of them was the object of the delicate adjusting care of which I have spoken. The conviction was of a boundless love that was yet individual, immediate, intimate. And that of necessity, while leaving to each individual his own proper freedom. The conviction had a universal quality.

Later, I happened upon two passages that seemed pertinent to my conviction. The one was from Plotinus, in which he explains the relation of the subjective element to the power outside and greater than ourselves by commenting on the *Timaeus*.[1]

' The Timaeus indicates the relation of this guiding spirit to ourselves : it is not entirely outside of ourselves; is not bound up with our nature; is not the agent in our action; it belongs to us as belonging to our Soul, but not in so far as we are particular beings living a life to which it is superior : take the passage in this sense and it is consistent; understand this Spirit otherwise and there is contradiction. And the description of the Spirit, moreover, as " the power which consummates the chosen life," is, also, in agreement with this interpretation; for while its presidency saves us from falling much deeper into evil, the only direct agent within us is something neither above it nor equal to it but under it : Man cannot cease to be characteristically Man.'

[1] *op. cit., Our Tutelary Spirit.* (See *The Spiritual Imperative*).

The other passage is from *The Revelations of Divine Love* [1]: ' And from that time that it was shewed I desired oftentimes to see clearly (*witten*) what was our Lord's meaning. And fifteen years after, and more, I was answered in my ghostly understanding, saying thus: *Wouldst thou witten thy Lord's meaning in this thing? Learn it well; Love was His meaning. Who shewed it thee? Love. What shewed He thee? Love. Wherefore shewed it He? For Love. Hold thee therein and thou shalt learn and know more in the same. But thou shalt never know nor learn therein other thing without end.*

VI

There are also Minute Particulars. A hint may come from anything. The smallest thing may speak to a man of the whole round world,[2] and the most casual sight convince him of the Universal Soul, which is above the antithesis of freedom and necessity. The swirling of a leaf in the wind may assure him of the Power whose centre is everywhere and circumference nowhere. The bend in a road, the careless shout of a gipsy, the greeting of a friend met by chance on a torn-up battle-field—a thousand ordinary happenings may so enlarge the portals of his spirit that his wonder embraces ' all-thing ' and he stands bareheaded without word of prayer.

' Who has not learnt, whatever the particular line of his studies, to discover in himself something

[1] *op. cit.*, p. 202.
[2] *cf.* Lady Julian, *op. cit.*, p. 26 : ' I saw God in a point.'

infinite? The conviction comes to some people with overwhelming force in the presence of Alpine scenery, or on catching sight of a distant horizon, or by contrast, in the contemplation of something slight and almost commonplace, such as a streamlet, or a field of snow, rendered magical by some simple effect of colour. To others this whisper from eternity comes with the sound of music or, strangely enough, after witnessing some unexpected touch of human nature while passing in the street.' [1]

The intuitions may be painful. They may be associated with apparent cruelty or the end-of-the-world crying of a child or a woman's suffering or any kind of seeming torture or enslavement. Yet the intuitions arising out of these painful particulars have an undertone of something which vindicates the supremacy of the good. They reflect in an inexpressible manner the Divine pity and indignation.

Minute Particulars were important to Blake. He gives account of them in a poem with the inspired title of *Auguries of Innocence*,[2] beginning,

> To see a World in a Grain of Sand
> And a Heaven in a Wild Flower,
> Hold Infinity in the palm of your hand
> And Eternity in an hour.

The painful side is very prominent:

> A Robin Redbreast in a Cage
> Puts all Heaven in a Rage
>
> . . . . . .
> He who shall hurt the little Wren
> Shall never be beloved by men.

and many other examples of animals, birds, human beings.

[1] *God, Man & Epic Poetry* by H. V. Routh, I, p. 4.
[2] Nonesuch, p. 118.

He knows how the two sides go together :

> Joy & Woe are woven fine,
> A Clothing for the Soul divine:

He is conscious of the undertone :

> Under every grief and pine
> Runs a joy with silken twine . .

[This is not the same as the ' cloud and the silver lining.' The silken twine of the joy is there all the time and present to the thought.]

And out of it all he gathers up a great thing :—

> God appears & God is light
> To those poor Souls who dwell in Night,
> But does a Human Form display
> To those who Dwell in Realms of day.

VII

When we come to the supreme experience we find men returning to the childish way. They bring along with them all that they have learned; *that* has been accepted, taken up into themselves, but their great words, Love, Beauty, Good, Truth, are like a little girl's doll : they are symbols of which the content or meaning is ineffable.

The end of seeing is knowing. Browning's oft-quoted line from *Abt Vogler*, ' The rest may reason and welcome; 'tis we musicians know,' has pertinence, because Browning's poems on music are not about music; they are about life. The knowledge does not come to musicians only or artists or poets; it comes to those who have learned to trust their intuitions, who accept that knowledge which is neither conceptual nor rational.

Richard Rolle tries to tell us what Love is. It is a Life, a Light, a Melody,[1] a Spiritual Drink :—

> Love is Life that lasts ay.[2]
> Raise me up to thy light
>   thy melody to hear.[3]
> Thy love shines day and night
>   that strongs me in this street.[4]
> Love is a ghostly wine
>   that makes men big and bold [5]
> Love is stalwart as death [6]

Arthur Clarke had a little aphorism : Love is the perfect of Live. Or again,

> Love is a singing bird,
>   Singing a note or two,
> When comes the third,
>   Love is thy due.

Beauty in Plotinus, as we have seen, is τὸ καλόν, all that is worthy of love and admiration. The beauty of the soul is to be made like unto God. And this happens ' when you find yourself true to your essential nature, wholly that only veritable Light . . .'

Socrates in the *Symposium* [7] modestly attributes to the wise woman of Mantinea the theory that visible beauty is the reflection in our earthly life of an eternal, unchangeable Beauty that can be perceived with the

---

[1] *cf. Ennead* vi, 9, 8 : ' thus a choir, singing set in due order about the conductor, may turn away from that centre to which all should attend; let it but face aright and it sings with beauty, present effectively. We are ever before the Supreme—cut off is utter dissolution; we can no longer be—but we do not always attend : when we look our term is attained; this is rest; this is the end of singing ill; effectively before Him, we lift a choral song full of God ' (trans. by Stephen MacKenna and B. S. Page : Medici Society).

[2] *op. cit.*, p. 245.   [3] p. 263.   [4] p. 270.   [5] p. 254.   [6] p. 255.

[7] W. R. M. Lamb's Edition of Plato, V, p. 76 (Loeb).

eye of the mind. By victory over the lower elements of Eros, and the pursuit of Beauty on ever higher and higher levels, its essence is at last in a sudden flash revealed, and the revelation is all rewarding.

Browning, considering a picture of *The Guardian Angel* by Guercino, Elizabeth being with him and his friend, Alfred Domett, present to his mind, concludes

> Oh, world as God has made it! All is beauty,
> And knowing this is love, and love is duty.

Plato in his VIIth Epistle declares his intention of publishing nothing on his Idea of the Good: ' There is no writing of mine on this subject nor ever shall be. It is not capable of expression like other branches of study; but as the result of long intercourse and a common life spent upon the thing, a light is suddenly kindled as from a leaping spark, and when it has reached the Soul, it thenceforward finds nourishment for itself.'

I have already referred to Isaac Penington's pregnant saying about Truth : '' Every truth is a shadow except the last. But every truth is substance in its own place, though it be but a shadow in another place. And the shadow is a true shadow and the substance a true substance.' After a common life spent upon the thing we come to perceive that everything has its proper truth. We do not reject the truth; we accept it. We only know that it is a shadow of the Ultimate Truth or Significance. We are convinced that the Truth, the Very Truth,[1] waits to be

---

[1] *cf. Ennead* vi. 9, 11 : ' for There his converse was not with image, not with trace [meaning ' shadow ' ?] but with the very Truth in the view of which all the rest is but of secondary concern.'

revealed, and that the recognition of every separate truth, which is substance in its own place, is a foreshadowing of the Truth.

The great words are interchangeable, apparently, and when all is said convey little except through some mirror in ourselves. ' Remember that there are parts of what it most concerns you to know which I cannot describe to you; you must come with me and see for yourselves.'

As I began with my experience as a little boy, listening enthralled to my father's reading of the *Ancient Mariner*—an experience, on the one side, of praying, and on the other, a revelation of beauty— I will close with another experience of forty years later. I was watching a dying woman, and I noted in her face the ravages of disease. She was unconscious, and in her last moments of consciousness had said to me, ' There must be no sense of hurry. There may be something to be seen or done even now.' I was standing at the foot of her bed, and I turned round and gazed at a portrait of her taken when she was a young woman. I could not help contrasting its clear beauty with the stricken face on the pillow. Then I looked back again, and the face on the pillow was infinitely—yes, infinitely—the most beautiful I have seen. And I thought : ' This is what she was meant to be. This is what she really is.'

It was an intuition that completed all else : that in the life of men, their actual bodily life here, without disregarding anything that men call evil, there is a beauty inexpressible and this inexpressible beauty is the truth of human existence.

And now, with the urgent reminder that Intuition is complementary to the exercise of reason and capacity and whatever else is properly called ' common sense ' in religion and life, I may sum up the results of this inquiry :

(1) The mode of apprehension necessary to the mystical life is Intuition, of which Vision and the Spiritual Imperative are more or less supernormal forms.

(2) Mysticism, in the traditional view, is a way of praying, and the ' mystical experience ' is the intuition of God as present.

(3) Mysticism, considered as an outlook, is a way of seeing the great things in the small things, and the ' mystical experience ' is the intuitive knowledge of the Great Thing.

(4) There is a mystical element of poetry, though the poet, as such, is not a mystic, in the traditional sense. In that sense he is, as Bremond calls him, a *mystique manqué*. The true poet, however, has always the mystical outlook; and so has everyone who recognizes the poetry of existence.

ACKNOWLEDGMENTS

ACKNOWLEDGMENTS

I HAVE acknowledged, in the text, my obligations to Miss Elizabeth Holmes, The Rev. Bertram Lester, S.S.M., and my brother, W. A. Brockington. I have also to thank the following: Dr. H. V. Routh, who read my first draft and criticised it to my great benefit and also made suggestions that I was eager to adopt; The Rt. Rev. the Lord Bishop of Liverpool, who, as Editor of the *Liverpool Review*, admitted a series of articles on ' modes of apprehension '; The Rt. Rev. W. F. Wentworth-Shields, Warden of St. Deiniol's Library, Hawarden; The Rev. M. W. T. Conran, S.S.J.E.; The Rev. Dr. M. W. Myres, to whom I am indebted for revision of proofs—and much else; Dr. W. Dallas Ross; Mr. Arthur Waugh; the late Mr. Richard Paden; and, for a service, the value of which the reader may estimate for himself, Sir Arthur Stanley Eddington. But none of these friends and helpers is responsible for anything in the way of theory or deduction or for any mistakes in information or faults of expression.

My chief debt is to R. E. B., for her vivid sympathy and devoted care.

Detailed references to sources are given in the footnotes. I have asked for and obtained the courteous sanction of owners of copyright material: M. Bernard Grasset, for permission to quote passages

from Abbé Henri Bremond's *Prière et Poésie;* Mr.
Geoffrey Keynes and the Nonesuch Press, for the
unrestricted use of *Poetry and Prose of William
Blake;* Mr. John Murray, for the right to quote from
his edition of the *Poetical Works of Robert
Browning;* the Oxford University Press, for a similar
right in respect of the *Poems of Gerard Manley
Hopkins, Gerard Manley Hopkins* by G. F. Lahey,
the *Oxford Book of English Mystical Verse,* chosen
by D. H. S. Nicholson and A. H. E. Lee, and Prof.
Ernest de Selincourt's *Wordsworth's Prelude;* the
Cambridge University Press, for permission to quote
from C. H. Sorley's *Marlborough and Other Poems;*
Mr. Thomas Baker, for passages from David Lewis's
translation of the *Ascent of Mount Carmel,* by St.
John of the Cross; Dom G. Bruno Hicks, Abbot of
Downside, and Messrs. Constable and Co., for the
use of Dom Cuthbert Butler's works, especially
Western Mysticism; Messrs Macmillan and Co., for
quotations from Rudolf Otto's *Mysticism East and
West;* Messrs. Duckworth and Co., for quotations
from *Outline-History of Greek Religion* by L. R.
Farnell; Messrs. Methuen and Co., for passages from
Lady Julian's *Revelations of Divine Love* and from
T. F. Knox's translation of the *Life of the Blessed
Henry Suso;* Jonathan Cape, Ltd., for extracts
from Hermann Keyserling's *Europe;* Ernest Benn,
Ltd., for a passage from W. Hale White's translation
of Spinoza's *Ethic;* Messrs. George Allen and Unwin,
for quotations from *A Short History of Quakerism,*
by E. B. Emmott; Messrs. P. J. and A. E. Dobell,
for passages from Thomas Traherne's *Centuries of*

Meditation; Messrs J. M. Dent and Sons, for quotations from Baron von Hügel's *Mystical Element of Religion;* Miss Frances Comper and the same publishers for quotations from Richard Rolle's Lyrics (*The Life of Richard Rolle,* etc.); the owner of the copyright of Stephen MacKenna's translation of Plotinus, published by the Medici Society, for the use of this translation in aid of my own efforts; Mr. George Bernard Shaw, and Messrs Constable and Co., for extracts from the Preface to Bernard Shaw's *Saint Joan;* Mr. G. K. Chesterton and Messrs. Chatto and Windus, for a passage from *A Short History of England* by G. K. Chesterton.

Some living poets have permitted me to quote from their works: Mr John Masefield, from ' The Dream,' *The Everlasting Mercy* and *Good Friday* (Heinemann); Prof. A. E. Housman, from *A Shropshire Lad* and *Last Poems* (Grant Richards) and from *The Name and Nature of Poetry* (Cambridge University Press); Mr Walter de la Mare (who is always most courteously ready to help me), from ' Hospital ' in *The Veil and Other Poems* (Constable); Mr Edmund Blunden, from *Halfway House* (Cobden-Sanderson); Mr T. S. Eliot, from *The Waste Land* (Faber and Faber).

I have not included a Bibliography, because my book is documented and because there are many bibliographies easily accessible to students.

My son, Paul, and his wife have compiled the Index.

A. A. B.

INDEX

INDEX